Vanished
MISSISSIPPI GULF COAST

Downtown Biloxi, after Hurricane Katrina.

Though the ground floor of this home along Highway 90 in Gulfport was gutted by Katrina's storm surge, a place was still found to fly the flag.

Vanished
MISSISSIPPI GULF COAST

BY JIM FRAISER   PHOTOGRAPHY BY RICK GUY AND JIM FRAISER

PELICAN PUBLISHING COMPANY
GRETNA 2006

The word "Pelican" and the depiction of a pelican are trademarks of Pelican Publishing Company, Inc.,and are registered in the U.S. Patent and Trademark Office.

Library of Congress Cataloging-in-Publication Data

Fraiser, Jim, 1954-
  Vanished Mississippi Gulf Coast / by Jim Fraiser ; photography by Rick Guy and Jim Fraiser.
      p. cm.
  ISBN-13: 978-1-58980-346-6 (hardcover : alk. paper)
  1. Gulf Coast (Miss.)—History, Local—Pictorial works. 2. Gulf Coast (Miss.)—Social life and customs—Pictorial works. 3. Historic buildings—Mississippi—Gulf Coast—Pictorial works. 4. Architecture—Mississippi—Gulf Coast—Pictorial works. 5. Gulf Coast (Miss.)—History—Pictorial works. I. Title.
  F347.G9F73 2006
  976.2—dc22
                                        2006010249

Printed in Singapore
Published by Pelican Publishing Company, Inc.
1000 Burmaster Street, Gretna, Louisiana 70053

For my daughters, Lucy and Mary Adelyn, and my wife, Carole, whose love for the Mississippi coast almost matches my affection for them—J. F.

For Haley and Alan—R. G.

Great Southern Golf Club, Gulfport. The original clubhouse (1910) sat in ruins after Hurricane Katrina washed over the beachfront course.

Contents

Whitecaps wash over Highway 49 just south of I-10 in Gulfport during Katrina.

Preface

Upon observing predictions that we were mired in a thirty-year cycle of more frequent and destructive hurricanes, I became concerned that my beloved Mississippi coast was due for another Camille-like hurricane that would devastate the region. Not long after Rick Guy and I produced *The Majesty of Eastern Mississippi and the Coast* for Pelican Publishing Company in 2004, multiple hurricanes ravaged Gulf Shores, Pensacola, and Punta Gorda. Convinced that time was running out for the historical structures lining Mississippi's beaches, I asked Pelican to allow us to revisit the coast and preserve for posterity its history, architecture, and culture as it had developed since the French landed at what is now Ocean Springs in 1699.

We finished the project just in time. Rick was taking his final photographs when Katrina struck. He rode out the storm in a hotel near Interstate 10. When the monster finally relented, and gulf waters receded, Rick made the same terrible discovery that we would all have no choice but to accept—Mississippi's coast, and many of her historic structures, lay in ruins. The twenty-six-mile length of the coast, and most historic structures located within a few blocks of the beach, had simply been wiped from the map. Worse, the loss of life exceeded even that wrought by category-five Camille's 1969 assault.

But Katrina failed in her efforts to dispirit the people inhabiting our coast. These were, after all, a people who had survived war, plague, and almost yearly hurricane onslaughts to build one of the nation's greatest vacation resorts and some of the loveliest, most intriguing towns and villages in America. But as they labor to rebuild their region, many cannot help but cast a wistful eye to the past, and to all they lost in Katrina's monstrous thirty-five-foot-tall tidal surges.

It is, therefore, for them that Rick and I offer this paean to the extraordinary history, architecture, and culture our coast people forged during their first 300 years. In so doing, we present the book just as we had originally conceived it, with the Mississippi Gulf Coast in all its unique and quirky glory, but with additional information as to damage suffered by the structures. We also offer this book as a reminder to the world of what the vanished Mississippi coast was before August 29, 2005, and, considering the unyielding spirit of her people, what it will surely be once again.

Acknowledgments

We gratefully acknowledge the assistance and support of the home-owners who allowed us access to their lovely homes; the chambers of commerce in each of the coastal towns who gave us much needed direction; the staffs of the Mississippi Department of Archives and History, especially Jennifer Baughn; the Hancock County Historical Society; coast historians Ray L. Bellande and Paul Estronza, without whom this book would not have been possible; and publisher Dr. Milburn Calhoun and editor Nina Kooij. We also acknowledge the great courage, endurance, and charity demonstrated by the people of the Mississippi Gulf Coast, who survived the wrath of Camille and her pred-ecessors, rebuilt the coast each time, and will do so again, despite Katrina's monstrous but failed efforts to defeat them.

Introduction

When they landed at what is now Ocean Springs in 1699, Iberville's French expedition immediately envisioned the Mississippi Gulf Coast as a land of extraordinary promise, despite the excessive humidity, boundless forests, occasionally hostile natives, and ubiquitous mosquitoes "which punctured the skin most savagely." The British never got a chance to land during the War of 1812, after a lady in Bay St. Louis fired a cannon at their warships, and American sailors in the Mississippi Sound delayed the Brits' advance to New Orleans just long enough for Gen. Andrew Jackson to prepare for the Battle of New Orleans. A half-century later, an invading Union fleet found Mississippi's still thinly populated coastal hamlets largely undefended, and ceased shelling Pass Christian only after a housewife and mother waved a bedsheet on her gulf-facing upper gallery to signal the town's "Bedsheet Surrender."

Mississippi's coast is as drenched in history as it is in sunshine on a midsummer's day and, even after Katrina, still offers an impressive array of historical structures to prove it. From Biloxi's Beauvoir, the Greek Revival-style raised cottage that served as the last residence of Confederate president Jefferson Davis, to Gulfport's Mission-style Dantzler House, home to one of Mississippi's most significant lumber-exporting families, coastal landmarks lined the beach highway and transported the visitor to bygone eras of unsurpassed luxury. However, after August 29, 2005, when Katrina destroyed or severely damaged 103,000 of the estimated 171,000 homes on Mississippi's coast, fewer of those historic structures stand than at any time since the Civil War.

There's never been any shortage of legend in these parts. The haunting strains of the ancient Pascagoula Indian death song may still be heard on the banks of Pascagoula's Singing River, while scholars continue to debate the impact of pirates like Jean Lafitte and Pierre Remaux on the region's people and economy.

The coast's architecture is no less legendary, preserved through the years in National Register-established Historic Districts with styles ranging from early French Colonial, West Indies, and Greek Revival to Twentieth-Century Victorian, Mission, and Bungalow. Pascagoula's Old Spanish Fort, erected in 1721, remains the oldest surviving residential structure in the lower Mississippi River valley, while Pass Christian's Ballymere was the oldest Creole cottage on the "West (Mississippi) Coast" until it was destroyed by Katrina.

Despite the occasional onslaughts of terrible hurricanes like a 1947 storm that "churned" Gulfport into the sea, 1969's Camille, which wiped Pass Christian from the map, and Katrina, which did $75 billion of damage and took an estimated 1,500 lives, coast people forged a unique, polyglot culture that is one part genteel small town and one part tourist mecca, with Las Vegas-style casinos and the longest man-made beach in the world. But this is also an art-lover's paradise, where locals and tourists alike revere the tradition of Ocean Springs' favorite son and America's most eccentric naturalist painter, Walter Anderson; the "Mad Potter of Biloxi," George E. Ohr; and Bay St. Louis's renowned folk artist, Alice Moseley.

The sign on one of the coast's preeminent seafood restaurants reads simply, *Like this, no place,* and those words surely apply to the entire Mississippi coast. Another signpost of the region's quirky but undeniable culinary excellence is the 500-year-old live oak, the Patriarch Oak, whose ancient branches still shade a marvelous French restaurant situated in one of Biloxi's oldest structures. That one popular Gulfport eatery garnished diners' plates with plastic houseflies surprises no one who expects the unexpected in this most charming of Southern locales.

But the most impressive aspect of the Mississippi Gulf Coast is not her history, architecture, or culture. It's her people, who have become both more flamboyant and more egalitarian than any citizenry this side of Australia. Perhaps it's the coast's Franco-Spanish influence so unfamiliar to most Anglo-American-founded towns, or the significant impact made by Native and African-Americans, who helped establish this region as one truly like no other.

Whatever the case, coast residents have endured three major wars, numerous devastating hurricanes, annual nineteenth-century yellow-fever epidemics, and almost every catastrophe unthinking man and merciless gods could devise. But after each disaster they have regrouped, reconsidered, and rebuilt, creating in the process a wide-open society where the locals revel in the good life, tourists are made to feel welcome, and all join together to "pass a real good time." Not even Katrina could dampen their spirit. They will rebuild the coast once again and make it once more one of the greatest places to live or visit that the Western Hemisphere has ever seen.

Vanished
MISSISSIPPI GULF COAST

Firemen checkout a demolished home off Beach Boulevard in Gulfport after Katrina.

Ocean Springs

No American adventure surpasses the one that gave birth to what is now the Mississippi Gulf Coast. That extraordinary episode, which American history records as the founding of a French settlement at Old Biloxi, or modern-day Ocean Springs, was as improbable a beginning as any since Columbus first sighted the New World. But even that beginning is not where this story starts.

History

Although Spanish explorer Hernando De Soto made earlier incursions (circa 1541) into what is now northern Mississippi, the first European to venture down the Mississippi River to its mouth was a Frenchman named Robert Cavelier, Sieur de la Salle. In 1682, La Salle, the intrepid leader of an expedition of fifty-six Frenchmen and ten native women, claimed the Mississippi River valley for France. However, that region had been home to Indian tribes such as the Choctaw, Chickasaw, Natchez, and Biloxi for longer than the nation of France had graced European maps.

Paleo-Indians had arrived in the area around 10,000 B.C. By A.D. 800, they were settling into villages of bark-roofed huts and raising corn, beans, pumpkins, and squash. By 1540, they had established organized societies with chiefdoms and priesthoods and created gigantic pyramidal mounds. There were nearly thirty thousand Muskogean-speaking natives in what is now Mississippi when De Soto arrived, almost two-thirds of whom were Choctaw. Coastal Indians hunted the primaeval forest for wildcat, cougar, wolf, fox, deer, squirrel, alligator, bear, wild pigs, and buffalo beneath towering magnolias, longleaf pine, and live oaks shrouded with gray Spanish moss. They fished streams that teemed with bass, bluegills, sunfish, and catfish and plied coastal waters for oysters, blue crab, speckled and white trout, redfish, mullet, flounder, sheepshead, and drum.

But the Choctaw and Chickasaw were not the only natives encountered by the Spanish and French. Mississippi's coastal region was also once home to other Muskogean-speaking peoples: the Houma, Ofo,

Pascagoula, Acolopissa, Capinan, Moctobi, Bayougoula, Mougoulacha, and Mobilians, as well as the Biloxi, a southern relative of the plains-riding Sioux.

It was to the Mougoulacha in 1685 that Henri de Tonti, an Italian adventurer in the service of France, had given a letter, with the request that they deliver it to the long-lost La Salle if he wandered into their village. Tonti would be disappointed; La Salle would be murdered by his own men after losing his way during an exploration of the land he had claimed. The loyal but despairing Tonti returned to a French-Canadian settlement in Illinois, and the Indians held his letter for fourteen years, until they delivered it to the next Frenchman they saw.

And this is really where the great gulf coast adventure begins. Pierre le Moyne, Sieur d'Iberville, eldest of the eleven Le Moyne brothers, had already achieved lasting fame in Canada before he ever left France for the gulf coast. A large man with blond hair and blue eyes, the thirty-five-year-old Iberville had captured an English warship using only twelve cannon and eleven men in bark canoes. He had saved Hudson Bay by repulsing three English ships and with a mere fourteen men had taken more than a hundred English prisoners.

Aware that the Spanish were moving on Florida and that the English were planning an excursion down the Mississippi to reverse La Salle's claims, Iberville convinced the French sovereign to let him establish a colony near the Mississippi's mouth. On October 24, 1698, he left Brest, France, with 200 mostly Canadian male colonists, headed for the Mississippi. He commanded one frigate, *La Badine,* with thirty guns and a French crew of 200, including his twenty-year-old brother, Jean Baptiste le Moyne, Sieur de Bienville, who served as midshipman. A second frigate, the thirty-gun *Le Marin,* was commanded by M. le Compte de Sugere, with a crew of 150 and another Le Moyne brother, Antoine Le Moyne, Jean de Sauvolle, serving as sublieutenant. The expedition was accompanied by *La Précieuse* and *L'Espérance,* two Norman fishing boats used solely for storage.

Upon arriving in St. Domingue, they met the fifty-gun ship, *Le François,* commanded by the Marquis de Chateaumerant, which escorted them to the coast by way of Cuba, Pensacola, and Mobile Bay. According to Iberville's journal, on February 10, 1699, the *François* anchored "a cannon's shot off [Ship Island] in 26 feet of water." On the thirteenth, Iberville and twelve men took two small boats, he a "Biscayan" rowboat and Sauvolle a bark canoe, and rowed ten miles from Ship Island toward the mainland to a spot where they found "plum trees in bloom; tracks of turkeys, partridges no bigger than quail, hares like the ones in France; [and] some rather good oysters." This location was likely near where Biloxi's antebellum mansion, Beauvoir, now stands.

Of the Biscayan boats, Iberville said with typical French wit, "it's a jolly business indeed to explore the sea coasts with longboats that are not big enough to keep to the sea . . . and are too big to approach a flat coast on which they run aground a half league off shore."

They soon discovered the natives. Despite offering enticements of knives, axes, glass beads, and "a little vermillion," the French were unable to persuade their uncertain hosts to come forth. Spying a group of Indians canoeing from Deer Island toward the mainland east of their position, Iberville gave chase along the shoreline. After landing at what is now Ocean Springs on the fourteenth, Iberville finally caught an old native man, too sick to run. He later captured a woman and gave her tobacco to take to her tribesmen.

The next day, several Biloxi ventured into the French camp. They were treated to various gifts and a French custom they would famously adopt for their own, known as smoking the peace pipe, or calumet. This particular pipe was three feet long with a bowl fashioned as a ship flying a fleur-de-lis flag. In honor of this meeting, Iberville named the beachhead, and their future settlement, after the Biloxi.

On the seventeenth, a Bayou-goula chief and twenty of his men met with the French, smoked the peace pipe, and "danced the calumet." While enjoying tobacco (all except Iberville, who hated it), Indian corn,

Deer Island, named by the French in 1699 for the abundant deer roaming it, is generally considered to be the loveliest of Mississippi's five barrier islands.

brandy, and much singing by both sides, the French reached a momentous accord with the Bayougoula, Biloxi, Pascagoula, and Acolopissa, which those tribes honored for the entire sixty-four years of French dominion on the coast.

On February 27, Iberville set out in search of the "Myssysyy" River, known to the coast Indians as the "Malbouchia." With Bienville, Sauvolle, and forty-eight men, including Father Douay, who had previously accompanied La Salle down the Mississippi, Iberville left in two Biscayans and two bark canoes loaded with sixteen casks of wine and supplies of flour and butter. They entered the great river on March 2, breaking through a mud bank into water only twelve feet deep. The next day, the explorers celebrated Mardi Gras from the bow of a longboat, giving prayers of thanks and offering wine to the celebrants.

Traveling upriver, Iberville met Indians who showed him a cloak of blue serge, which they had received as a gift from Tonti years earlier. Weeks later, while returning downriver, Sauvolle received a letter from the Mougoulacha, dated April 20, 1685, from Tonti to La Salle. It read in part:

> Upon this information I came downriver with 25 Frenchmen. . . .
> All the nations have danced the calumet for me. These are people
> who have feared us in the extreme since you destroyed this village.
> I shall end by telling you that I am greatly grieved that we are going
> back, having suffered the misfortune of failing to find you. . . . I am
> not without hope that God will give you marked success. . . . This I
> wish with all my heart.

As Tonti had grieved the loss of his friend, so too did the Le Moynes encounter hardships in the New World. Chief among these were dysentery and "musquitos," which, as related by expedition carpenter Penicaut, "the Indians call Marangouins, which puncture the skin very savagely." Nevertheless, they returned to Ship Island on March 31, where Iberville began planning a semi-permanent beachhead.

Iberville established his temporary settlement on the east side of Biloxi Bay at "Old Viloxy" (present-day Ocean Springs) by laying a garrison's foundation on April 8, 1699. He named it Fort Maurepas, after the French Minister of Marine (Navy), Jerome Phelypeaux de Maurepas, Comte (Earl) de Pontchartrain.

Fort designer Remy Reno built bastions, palisades, living quarters, and warehouses from indigenous oak, hickory, and pine. Iberville armed the eighty-man fort with twelve cannon from *La Badine* and *Le Marin*. His inventory, compiled after the fort's completion on April 25, included a bull, cows, hogs, and pea and corn seed plus squandered provisions of rotted peas, spoiled bacon, sour dustlike flour, two barrels of soured wine, and barrels of olive oil and brandy lost to leakage.

Fort Maurepas, Front Beach Drive. This was a 1980s reconstruction of the fort that was built in 1699 by Iberville, believed to be 100 yards west of the site of the original fort. It was severely damaged by Hurricane Katrina in 2005.

These losses proved prophetic as the colony immediately fell on hard times. Iberville left for France days later, leaving Sauvolle in charge with Bienville second in command. The colony was unable to overcome the mosquitoes, snakes, alligators, yellow fever, and food and water shortages that plagued it, and Iberville dismantled the fort and moved the capital of his settlement to Mobile in 1702.

This failure in no way diminishes the accomplishments of these intrepid adventurers. They sailed across a vast ocean in tiny wooden boats and established a beachhead in a hostile new world against all possible odds. They eventually dominated the region thanks to the Le Moyne brothers, including Iberville the explorer, and Sauvolle, who, as governor blunted a 1700 Spanish strike force by wining and dining the Spanish governor and escorting him back to Pensacola. Bienville, with five men in two bark canoes, bluffed English captain Louis Bank and his ten-gun ship into turning around and leaving the Mississippi River to the French. The river bend where this occurred, near present-day New Orleans, is known to this day as "English Turn." Bienville later founded New Orleans in 1718.

Tonti returned in 1700 and helped maintain friendly relations with the natives. Admired by them for his iron hand (literally—his real hand was blown off by a grenade during a battle in Europe), exceptional courage, and supposed magical powers, Tonti once tricked hostile braves into sparing his life by telling them they shouldn't kill a man who carried their pictures close to his heart, then proving it by showing them a mirror in his pocket.

These were irrepressible French souls, like one Le Sueur, a geologist who left the settlement in 1700 with twenty-five men, traveled to Sioux country in present-day Minnesota, and returned from his 2,000-mile canoe trip with the first commercial cargo (beaver pelts) to descend the Mississippi. Lawrence DeGraff, the buccaneer captain and famed soldier who escorted Iberville's party from St. Domingue to the coast in 1699, may best encapsulate the flamboyance, resilience, and hardiness of these great discoverers. DeGraff was "tall and straight, handsome, but not effeminate," as one contemporary wrote. He continued:

His hair was of a golden blonde, and a moustache after the Spanish fashion that admirably became him. A better canonier was never known.... He was prompt, bold and determined. To resolve, undertake and execute were to him the same. He was perfectly intrepid in danger, but impatient, passionate and swore too much. ... He was proficient in music, with a most melodious voice. Thus he distinguished himself by his politeness and refined tastes, no less than by his audacity, and wherever he went crowds gathered around to satisfy themselves whether he was a man or demi-god.

When the capital was moved to Mobile, only a few settlers chose to stay behind to reside alongside the natives in Old Biloxi. The capital briefly returned to the area in 1719, but the French established a new capital across the bay the next year, a garrison called Fort Louis, at present-day Biloxi, probably near where the Biloxi Lighthouse now stands on Highway 90.

Of the settlers remaining in Old Biloxi, one was Cadet LaFontaine, who married one of the twenty-three "Cassette Girls," young French women with small cases (*cassettes*) in which they carried their trousseaus in anticipation of marriage, who came to Mobile on June 22, 1704, under the protection of Sister Jeane Marbe on the French frigate, *Le Pélican.* LaFontaine's bride, Françoise, later gave birth to Auguste, who married an Indian native named Catherine Nantes Perrache. Perrache was subsequently known as the "Widow" LaFontaine, the grandame to numerous Ocean Springs descendants.

The tiny fishing settlement was ruled from a distance until 1763, when England took over. The English held dominion until 1779, when Spain acquired the colony. In 1812 the United States annexed the region, and Mississippi achieved statehood in 1817. However, the settlement enjoyed no real growth until the 1830s, when the wharf at the foot of the town's first street, Jackson Avenue, became a regular refueling stop on the New Orleans to

Garrard's Bayou House, 1119 Iberville Street (1890). This one-and-a-half-story Colonial Revival wood-frame house with a unique front window scheme and rear, enclosed dogtrot is located in the heart of the Marble Springs area.

Mobile steamboat run. Henrietta Porter opened the community's first hotel on Jackson Avenue in the 1830s, which offered haven to New Orleanians escaping their city's annual yellow-fever epidemics.

Despite this progress, by 1850 there were fewer than two hundred whites and only fifty-two bondsmen residing in the area. Three years later, the fifteen families in the region named their community Lynchburg, after a prominent mill operator, George Lynch. Obviously, the name did not last.

During an 1852 excavation for the foundation of a mill, springs containing iron oxide and sulfureted hydrogen were discovered a half-mile from the eastern shore of Biloxi Bay. The most important of these were the Marble Springs, located in the area of present-day Iberville Street. Although the natives had enjoyed the springs' medicinal qualities for centuries, naming them "E-ca-na-cha-ha," or "holy springs," it wasn't until Rev. P. P. Bowen discovered them, and New Orleans physician William G. Austin advocated their use, that white residents began exploiting them as a tourist attraction. Other important springs included the sulfur springs in the Indian Springs area and the warm mineral springs adjacent to the L & N Railroad Depot. The springs-driven tourist industry prompted the local government in 1854 to rename their town Ocean Springs.

The mineral springs boom led to the 1853 erection of the Ocean Springs Hotel by Dr. Austin and his

Winklejohn Home, 414 Martin Avenue (1840). This one-story Greek Revival cottage was once the sanatorium of Dr. William G. Austin, an advocate of local mineral springs. It features a five-bay facade with an undercut gallery and classically detailed entrance. It was damaged by Katrina but is repairable.

Anthony's Restaurant, 1217 Washington Avenue (1850). The core of this building was once an Indian Springs boardinghouse with marble baths. It was later fashioned into a restaurant.

mother-in-law, Henrietta Porter. It survived five hurricanes, yellow-fever epidemics, and the Civil War, until it burned to the ground in 1905.

Thanks largely to the railroad that brought New Orleans and Chicago tourists by the hundreds every summer, Ocean Springs prospered and its population increased from 600 in 1878 to 2,000 in 1915. Among the visiting Chicagoans were Mr. and Mrs. James Charnley, and their friend, architect Louis Sullivan. Sullivan and one of his draftsmen, Frank Lloyd Wright, designed for the Charnleys a collection of shingle-clad residential structures, including *T*-shaped bungalows and an octagonal guest cottage, sheltered by live oaks. The Charnley summer residence, which had been restored in 1930, was destroyed by Katrina.

Ocean Springs was incorporated in 1892 and, after the springs industry declined, enjoyed an economy based on year-round fishing, pecan cultivation (including Charles E. Pabst's nurseries), and orange production (led by Hernan D. Money's citrus orchards).

With these successful ventures, the region ultimately became Americanized, although some quaint French customs survived. These included the *lagniappe,* or small gift of candy or cookie given by storekeepers to kids running errands, and the *shivaree,* or pot-and-pan-banging, cowbell-ringing serenade for a remarrying widow.

Architecture

Ocean Springs boasts six historical districts with homes constructed in a variety of architectural styles. These include the Old Ocean Springs Historic District (1830-1935), the core around which the town developed, and the Shearwater Historic District (1850-1984), where world-renowned Shearwater Pottery and Walter Anderson's primitive-style art were born. The districts' prominent styles include the French-influenced raised cottage Bel Vue, the monumental Neo-classical Revival O'Keefe House, and the Hansey-Dickey House, a blend of the Prairie and Italian Renaissance styles.

Bel Vue, 810 Iberville Street (1827). This cottage was built by New Orleans developer and publisher George Cox, in the raised West Indian Colonial style with an inset gallery on brick piers. It is part of the Marble Springs Historic District.

O'Keefe House, 911 Porter (1906). This residence was built by Jeremiah O'Keefe with a full, two-story inset gallery and six Corinthian columns. It later became a restaurant and then a funeral parlor.

Other Ocean Springs architectural styles include the Greek Revival, which was favored by mid-nineteenth-century New Orleanians escaping yellow fever and exemplified in the Widmer House and the Winklejohn Home.

Queen Anne Revival cottages were popular between 1880 and 1910 during the advent of railway-opened mineral-springs tourism prosperity. The multigabled Saxon Home and the cross-gable-roofed Charbonnet House are prime examples.

From 1910 to 1930, as the town assumed a middle-income residential tone, Craftsman- and Bungalow-style homes predominated, with their wide-open eaves, broad low roofs, and pier

Hansey-Dickey House, 112-A Shearwater Drive (1905). Built on the coast's highest point, this home features Prairie-style elements, which include undulating parapets, a continuous gallery parapet cap, heavy entablature, small cornice, and heavy roof. The scored stucco facade and undercut *U*-shaped gallery are of the Italian Renaissance style. The house was severely damaged by Katrina.

Widmer House, 520 Jackson Avenue (1856). This Greek Revival shotgun house featured a three-bay facade of two French doors and a side hall. It was destroyed by Katrina.

Saxon Home, 318 Jackson Avenue (1900). This two-story house features a Z-shaped one-story porch with chamfered posts and a sawn balustrade.

Charbonnet House, 513 Front Beach Drive (1890). This Queen Anne-style home with a hip-roofed porch was severely damaged by Katrina.

Halstead Place, 545 Front Beach Drive (1910). This home was built in the Greek Revival style and rebuilt in Craftsman style in 1925 with wrap-around undercut gallery and gable-on-hip roof. It was destroyed by Katrina.

Terrace Hill, 418 Martin Avenue (1925). Built in the formal Bungalow style, this home is a symmetrical one-story block with an enclosed full-width porch supported by clustered columns. It was severely damaged by Katrina.

foundations. Examples include the Halstead Place and the smaller version located at 208 Washington Avenue (circa 1911).

Other interesting structures are the High Victorian Gothic St. John's Episcopal Church, the Cochran-Cassanova (1880) planter's cottage at 900 Robinson Street, and the Palfrey Estate at 1025 Lover's Lane, a wood-frame house with eight-bay screen-enclosed galleries built in 1875.

Culture

Ocean Springs relives its momentous founding every spring with the annual Landing of d'Iberville at the reconstructed Fort Maurepas, replete with children's pet parades, a historic ball and pageant, and a reenacted landing. Shops on Washington Avenue and Government and Robinson streets in the old downtown district offer art, antiques, pottery, local crafts, and authentic French pastry in a manner that suits the town's reputation as the quirkiest spot on the "East (Mississippi) Coast." A perfect example of Ocean Springs' personality is the shop on Government known as Art Who?, named for the occasion when visiting artist Andy Warhol, exasperated with a dowager's repeated expressions of devotion to art, finally asked, "Art who?"

Martha's Tea Room at 715 Washington Avenue offers an English-style tearoom in a Victorian setting. Tasty seafood and choice steaks were served for years at Anthony's Under the Oaks, nestled among 400-year-old oaks overlooking Fort Bayou at 1217 Washington Avenue, and at Jocelyn's, where a sign appropriately reads, *Like this, no place.* The place to stay is the Gulf Hills Hotel at 13701 Paso Road, established in 1927 with its own championship golf course. The hotel once served as a hideout for Al Capone and a summer escape for Elvis Presley. Most downtown structures were flooded but not destroyed by Katrina.

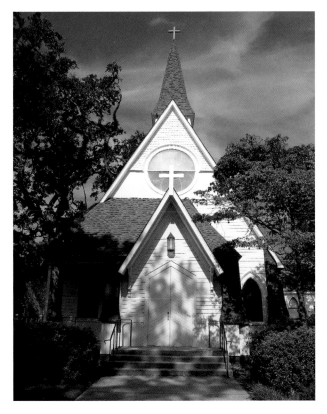

St. John's Episcopal Church, 711 Porter (1891). This was built from a Louis Sullivan design.

A stuffed toy peeks out from a broken wall beside a damaged apartment complex in Ocean Springs.

Jocelyn's, Highway 90. *Like this, no place.*

Perhaps the highpoint of Ocean Springs culture was the Shearwater Historic District, a veritable artist colony where Shearwater Pottery and the Walter Anderson cottage were located. Situated on twenty-four acres of wooded land overlooking the Mississippi Sound, the cottage was the 1920s home to Mississippi's greatest artist, Walter Anderson, and his brothers, potter Peter Anderson and painter and ceramist James McConnell Anderson. Walter's Greek Revival Vernacular, one-story, wood, raised cottage was built in 1850 as slave quarters on the Tiffen Estate. There, he painted his mural illustrating the 104th Psalm, "Creation at Sunrise," on the walls and ceiling of a "little room." That structure was damaged by Katrina but is under repair.

The informal grouping of 1930 one-story gable-roofed, board-and-batten buildings on brick piers was where Peter Anderson designed and produced his widget figurines and decorated pottery, the sale of which helped fund his brother's artwork. The *T*-shaped Shearwater Pottery Gallery was the exhibit area for the family's work, which included pieces by the Anderson brothers and their mother, New Orleans artist Annette McConnell Anderson. Fairhaven, or the Tiffen-DePass House, built in 1850 in the Greek Revival Vernacular style with a shed-roofed full-width gallery across the south facade, was the home Mrs. Anderson purchased for her family to reside, study, and work together in seclusion during the 1920s. It was destroyed by Katrina.

The Anderson legacy is alive and well in Ocean Springs, as may be seen in the collection at the Walter Anderson Museum of Art downtown, quite simply Mississippi's finest art museum. Shearwater Pottery was destroyed by Katrina, but the collection has been removed to the O'Keefe Cultural Center. Every first weekend in November, during the annual Peter Anderson Arts and Crafts Festival, locals and visitors alike revel in the legacy of an artist colony like no other in the Deep South.

Shearwater Pottery. These pieces are of the design made famous by Peter Anderson. Much of his pottery was destroyed by Katrina.

Walter Anderson Museum, 510 Washington Avenue. This houses art by Ocean Springs native Walter Anderson.

Pascagoula River, known in Indian mythology as the "Singing River." Here star-crossed lovers met their fates centuries before Romeo and Juliet.

Pascagoula

Iberville initially planned a temporary settlement in the New World near the mouth of the Pascagoula River. Though he eventually decided to build Fort Maurepas at Old Biloxi, where deeper water offered his ships better access, he soon returned to the area to trade with the Pascagoula and Biloxi natives. This region would eventually fly eight flags of the nations that would claim it, but it was truly legendary long before Europeans ever saw it.

History

The most famous area legend is the Singing River myth, centered on the pulchritudinous Pascagoula River, which then, as now, flowed through southern plains and marshland until it emptied into the gulf. Altama, son of the Pascagoula chief, fell in love with Anola, a lovely Biloxi maiden, but the latter tribe's fierce leader, Otanga, objected to the match. The Pascagoula fought bravely for their favorite son and his bride-to-be but found they could not hope to prevail against such great numbers. Chanting their death song, the entire tribe preceded the star-crossed lovers into the Pascagoula's depths, making the ultimate sacrifice to true love. Locals and visitors alike still hear their mournful dirge echoing between the Pascagoula's banks on certain summer nights. Even science has abetted the myth by confirming that a strange sound, likened to that of swarms of bees or strains of a harp, may be heard by those harkening their ears to the music of the "Singing River."

The lands on Pascagoula Bay (now North Pascagoula) were ceded in 1718 to Madame De Chaumont, a favorite of King Louis XIV. One of her first colonists was her brother, Joseph de la Pointe, who had arrived at Fort Maurepas in 1715. He erected a plantation on the back bay between 1718 and 1726. It was destroyed by a 1772 hurricane, its only surviving remnant—La Pointe's carpenter shop—now misnamed the Old Spanish Fort.

Lady Chaumont populated her colony in 1721 with 300 disreputable Frenchmen, 20 slaves, and 80 women from Parisian jails. The

29

Old Spanish Fort, 4602 Fort Street (1721). This is the oldest surviving residential structure in the lower Mississippi River valley. It sustained porch damage from Katrina.

colony survived the first year thanks to wheat-growing skills learned from the Pascagoula, whose name meant "bread people." Even so, the colony would never have succeeded but for the 1730 arrival of German immigrant Hugo Ernestus Krebs, whose descendants finally established a viable settlement.

Krebs eventually obtained La Pointe's plantation through marriage, and it prospered so well that his settlement soon became known as Krebsville. His son, Franz, invented an early cotton gin but failed to patent or mass market it. The Krebs family crafted boats in their backyard as early as 1772, launching an industry that would culminate with Ingalls Shipyard a century and a half later. Of the names of prominent early settlers such as Chaumont, La Pointe, Delmas (a Spanish immigrant), Graveline (a Canadian who established a settlement near the present-day location of the house known as Oldfields), and Rillieux (the French great-grandfather of renowned artist Degas), Krebs is most often heard in present-day Pascagoula.

Area lands passed to the English in 1763 but were handed to the Spanish in 1780 by virtue of the Franco-Spanish victory at the Battle of Baton Rouge, led by Capt. Vincent Rillieux. Venturesome Spaniards such as Valentine Delmas helped settle the region, but an 1810 revolution left it firmly in the hands of the newly founded Lone Star Republic of West Florida. What is now Pascagoula was subsequently included in the Mississippi Territory in 1812.

After helping to stave off the British, who occupied Horn Island during the War of 1812, the twenty families in the region welcomed Mississippi statehood in 1817. This brought in enterprising Americans such as engineer and eventual postmaster Louis Frederic, who arrived in 1820 and laid out the town's older streets of Scranton, Delmas, and Frederic in 1829. But despite the establishment of a port in 1840, the region saw little growth during the antebellum era apart from the sawmills established by Thomas Rhodes and William Dantzler.

During the Civil War, the Fourth Regiment of Louisiana and various local militia, including the Twiggs Rifles and Alfred Lewis's Live Oaks

Oldfields, 1901 Waters Edge Drive, Gautier (1849). This home was built by planter, politician, and Confederate colonel Alfred Lewis in the Greek Revival style, with a steeply pitched roof and full-front undercut gallery.

A. F. Dantzler House, Griffin Street, Moss Point (1906). Built in the Queen Anne style, this home rests on brick foundation piers and has an octagonal dormer tower, tent roof, and bracketed cornice. The chimneys with banding and the undercut gallery are also typical of that style.

Rifles, defended the area from Yankee invaders. On April 9, 1863, a company of 160 African-American Union soldiers stationed at Ship Island won the Pascagoula beachhead and raised a Federal flag over the East Pascagoula Hotel. They were eventually driven off, and Grant's forces did not occupy the town until early 1865.

The New Orleans, Mobile & Chattanooga Railroad began service to Pascagoula in 1870 at a depot on Delmas Street. Other nearby communities, such as Moss Point, just north of Pascagoula, and Gautier, formerly West Pascagoula, also began to prosper thanks to the lumber industry. The Dantzler Lumber Company, founded in 1877 by L. M. Dantzler, soon became one of south Mississippi's wealthiest corporations. By 1880, Pascagoula's port was shipping 60 million board feet of lumber per year.

In 1890 the tourist trade arrived, and the Pascagoula Hotel, with several hundred rooms for a thousand guests, proved one of the largest in the South. Another was the elegantly furnished Cottage by the Sea. Typical of turn-of-the-twentieth-century Pascagoula taverns was Randall's Tavern.

In 1893, Pascagoula boasted a burgeoning seafood industry, with arguably the largest and best-tasting oysters in the country. One private bed produced 100,000 barrels of the bivalves

Cottage by the Sea, 1205 Beach Boulevard (1872). Sea captain Charles Boster built this cottage as part of an exquisitely appointed resort hotel complex, considered one of the South's finest in that day. The one-story raised cottage featured an asbestos shingle roof with barrel tiles. It was destroyed by Katrina.

Randall's Tavern, 919 Beach Boulevard (1900). This tavern was damaged by a 1906 hurricane and converted to a residence in 1913. The two-story frame building featured an asphalt shingle-clad double-pitched roof and gallery. It was destroyed by Katrina.

per year. The town also produced the coast's first shrimp cannery in 1878.

But it would be the shipbuilding trade that would put Pascagoula on the map. Names such as Krebs, Delmas, Dantzler, Blanchard, and Frentz dominated the letterheads of shipbuilding firms that produced schooners, tugs, and barges during the timber and shipbuilding boom from 1874 to 1917. The International Shipbuilding Company launched the first all-steel vessel in 1917, but that achievement was topped in 1940 when Ingalls Shipbuilding Corporation launched the *Exchequer,* the world's first all-welded ship. Even this paled in comparison to Ingalls' 1955 achievement, when the nuclear power division produced two nuclear submarines, the *Sculpin* and the *Snook,* in the 158-acre shipyard. A 1968 U.S. Navy contract with Ingalls included a $2.14 billion work order for thirty destroyers, which would make up the backbone of America's modern fleet.

Architecture

The town's oldest section, now the Front Street Historical District (1820-1910), has several Greek Revival-style homes adapted to vernacular coast tastes, including the John B. Delmas House. However, the Victorian Vernacular was the town's dominant architectural style in the nineteenth century, and the California Bungalow style predominated in the modern era.

Memorable Pascagoula structures include Bellevue, where visiting poet Henry Wadsworth Longfellow supposedly penned "The Building of the Ship," a poetic description of a shipyard in "Pascagoula's sunny bay." This one-and-a-half-story wood-frame raised cottage was built by Capt. Daniel S. Graham of New Orleans. It was purchased in 1940 by Robert Ingalls, owner of Ingalls Shipbuilding Corporation. The home's full-width front gallery supported by square columns and surmounted by a full entablature, as well as its wide central hallway with large square rooms to each side, are characteristic of the Greek Revival style, while the double entrance stairways with iron grillwork handrails, and lower-story brick construction, with wood frame above and raised basement below, are coast vernacular elements.

A significant French-influenced Greek Revival structure was the Martin-Chastant House, generally considered to be the best example of lower Mississippi River valley regional architecture in Pascagoula. It had a full-width front double gallery supported by square Doric posts, double-leaf French doors, two rear *cabinets* (small storage rooms), and a flanking *loggia* (roofed open gallery).

In nearby Gautier (pronounced "Go-shay") stands the Greek Revival-style Old Place

John B. Delmas House, 2916 Front Street (1850). This home was built in the Greek Revival style but using Creole construction techniques such as a wide, low gallery and high foundation piers. The prominent Delmas family arrived in Pascagoula in 1800. This home suffered flood damage during Katrina.

Bellevue, 3401 Beach Boulevard (1854). This was also known as the Longfellow House, after the poet.

Stairs climb to a devastated structure along Beach Boulevard in Pascagoula. Katrina damaged or destroyed many beachfront homes.

Plantation House, considered by some to be built near the place that Iberville almost erected Fort Maurepas. It was constructed by Fernando Upton Gautier in 1856 for his wife, Judy, "to last as long as his love." The broad surrounding galleries with French doors and slender colonettes demonstrate its builder's taste for French design.

Three Queen Anne-style homes built during the 1899 lumber boom are the Nelson House, the Hughes House, and the Herrick House. Cobbler and dry goods merchant John C. Nelson built his gable-ended, wood-frame home atop raised brick piers. All three homes suffered only minor damage from Katrina.

Merchant William Hughes built his picturesque home with a pyramidal roof, cross gable on three elevations, and a multifaced conical

Martin-Chastant House, 2903 Beach Boulevard (1851). The home was destroyed by Katrina.

Nelson House, 2434 Pascagoula (1899). The home features a wraparound gallery.

Hughes House, 2425 Pascagoula Street (1899). Subsequent owner Claude Delmas won international fame for developing the Delmas and Schley pecan.

Herrick House, 2503 Pascagoula Street (1899).

Tabor House, 520 Live Oak (1905). A Tulane graduate and Mason, Dr. Tabor served in Cuba as personal physician to General Shafter in the Spanish-American War.

St. Mary's by the River, 3855 River Road (1925). The chapel includes a tabernacle for the Blessed Sacrament and a carved shrine to St. Mary the Virgin.

All that is left of this beachfront Pascagoula home is the slab and roof. The rest was washed away in the storm surge.

tower topped by a weathervane. Hughes' partner, Capt. Lemuel Herrick, hired John Stone to design his own two-story frame house with multiple gables, a tall slender chimney, a conical roof tower, and decorative wood shingles.

The Tabor House, located at the corner of Live Oak and Frederic streets, is the town's best example of a Dutch Colonial Revival residence. Dr. Joseph Tabor built this home with a picturesque gambrel roof, asymmetrical massing, decorative window lights, and wraparound porch with Doric columns.

St. Mary's by the River, in Moss Point, is Mississippi's only recorded example of a private residence designed and built to include a complete chapel. Of the eclectic "country house" style, it features Tudor and Mediterranean characteristics, as envisioned by architect Martin Shepard. Built for Sister Anne Christine Abercrombie, an Episcopal nun who took her novitiate in the New York community of St. Mary, the structure includes a twelve-by-twenty-foot chapel with a hand-carved German altar and Tiffany windows.

Culture

Pascagoula is the Mississippi Gulf Coast's ground zero for annual festivals and parades. Their Mardi Gras parades are among the state's most extravagant, and the Mississippi Gulf Coast Blues Festival rivals those presented in the legendary Mississippi Delta. The July 4th Fireworks event at Beach Park offers a grand celebration of the country's birthday, while the November Veterans Day Parade annually honors America's finest in magnificent style. October's Annual Jackson County State Fair is one of Mississippi's three remaining free fairs, and the downtown Christmas Parade concludes Pascagoula's seasonal festivities.

Downtown Pascagoula has several intriguing eateries, including Scranton's Restaurant, in the historic Number 1 Old Fire Station and City Hall, offering a fantastic rock-shrimp lunch special. Nellie's Tea Room at 707 Krebs Avenue serves specialty sandwiches and homemade pies that are "to die for," and the milkshakes at Edd's Drive Inn at 3834 Market Street reign supreme on the coast. These structures were flooded by Katrina but survived.

Pascagoula's history lives at the oldest surviving residential structure in the lower Mississippi River valley, the La Pointe-Krebs House at 4602 Fort Street. More famously (albeit incorrectly) known as the Old Spanish Fort, this former carpenter's shop was probably erected in 1721. An adjacent building houses era artifacts and representative displays of frontier life in French-dominated eighteenth-century North America.

Shephard State Park in Gautier, with park trails, a disc (Frisbee) golf course, soccer fields, and campgrounds, is nestled in the heart of Singing River country. Golf legends and duffers alike enjoy Gautier's Shell Landing Golf Club, one of Mississippi's top-five, public-access, championship-caliber courses.

For the naturalist, the "East (Mississippi) Coast" offers an abundance of bird, gator, and flower watching. A Moss Point airboat tour covers 105 acres of swamps, including the oldest gator farm in Mississippi, where fourteen-foot alligators and endangered birds bask in the coastal sun. The Mississippi Sandhill Crane National Wildlife Refuge in Gautier is both the 20,000-acre home of the endangered crane and the location of a unique wet pine savanna habitat with nature and hiking trails offering spectacular views of wildflowers, pitcher plants, sundews, and orchids.

Biloxi

A monstrous hurricane practically destroyed the French settlement at Biloxi in 1723. Almost 250 years later, Hurricane Camille, one of the worst hurricanes to strike the North American mainland in modern recorded history, demolished Biloxi and much of the western Mississippi coast. Neither storm succeeded in preventing this city's resilient denizens from establishing Biloxi (pronounced "buh-*luck*-see") as a shining star in the Mississippi Gulf Coast's constellation of prime vacation destinations.

History

From the very start, France's coastal colony at Old Biloxi endured unrelenting hardship. Its governor, Sauvolle, died in 1701. Along with its precious cargo of "Cassette Girls," the *Pélican* brought yellow fever in 1704, which claimed the life of the previously invincible Henri de Tonti. Iberville died in Havana in 1706, four years after he had moved the capital to Mobile. A particularly destructive hurricane drove the government back to Old Biloxi in 1719, but the bursting of promoter John Law's Mississippi Bubble forced yet another relocation in 1721, this time to the uncompleted Fort Louis, at present-day Biloxi.

This beachside flag display shows the many nations that have claimed Biloxi since the French arrived in 1699.

A letter to the French Ministry of Marine from M. le Blonde de la Tour, the Biloxi engineer who designed the original street plan for New Orleans, helps explain

39

Bienville's 1721 move from Ocean Springs (Old Biloxi) to "New Biloxi." "Besides the very bad air," de la Tour griped, "nearly 500 to 600 persons having died there in five to six months, and in spite of the cold weather that we have now, others are dying there every day; the very marshy water and in summer there is none at all; all this made me decide, gentlemen, to go on the very next day to visit the situation of New Biloxi which is very advantageous."

The relief offered by the eighty more "Cassette Girls" who arrived from France on *La Badine* in 1721 under the care of three Ursuline nuns was reversed by the 1723 hurricane, which flattened Biloxi and Pascagoula. Fed up with the coast, Bienville moved the seat of colonial government to New Orleans in 1726, where he busied himself enforcing his new Black Code for slaves and suffered continuous conflict with officious French bureaucrat Antoine de Cadillac. When the last French troops left Biloxi the following year, the town slipped into a slumber that lasted almost a century and a half.

By 1800, Biloxi had a population of 420 French Creoles, subsisting on fish and a few crops, fighting with the natives, raising cattle, and scratching out a living from production of pitch and tar. The first American land claims were made by the Ladners and Carquettes in 1814, and the town was incorporated in 1838. When the Catholic Church organized there in 1842, thanks in part to the arrival of hundreds of Irish fleeing their country's Potato Famine, Biloxi's residents took the necessary strides to put their hometown on the map.

They began by establishing tourist-friendly hotels, such as the Madame Pradat, Shady Grove Hotel, and Nixon Hotel. The only era structure still standing is the Magnolia Hotel, built for German

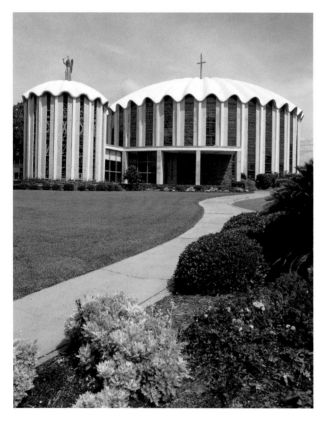

St. Michael's Catholic Church, 177 First Street (1964). Dedicated in the Diocese of Biloxi, the church's roof is made of crushed seashells, and its stained-glass windows depict the apostles as fishermen. It was severely damaged by Katrina but miraculously spared when a casino carried by the storm surge split apart and landed on both sides of the church.

businessman John Hohn. The two-story structure with brick-between-posts construction and encircling galleries was moved 150 yards north of the beach to its present location in 1969, after barely surviving Hurricane Camille. In the 1840s, its 6,000 annual visitors sampled outstanding cuisine while enjoying summer breezes in veranda rocking chairs, paying a mere two dollars a day or ten dollars a week for luxurious vacationing.

The coast's most famous landmark, the fifty-three-foot-tall, cast-iron Biloxi Lighthouse, was built at a cost of $12,000. "Manned" by women keepers from 1867 to 1929, it is the only lighthouse ever to be situated on the median of a United States highway,

The many grand antebellum homes lining Biloxi's beach included the Greek Revival-style Beauvoir, the French Colonial-style Hermann House, and the Southern Colonial Revival-style double-galleried Tullis-Toledano House.

While these gracious homes attracted favorable attention to the area in the 1850s, Biloxi received unwelcome attention during the Civil War, as Yankee soldiers and Union fleets invaded the coast in 1861. Biloxians had begun building Fort Twiggs on Ship Island in 1859, where their Biloxi Rifles served under seventy-one-year-old Gen. David Twiggs. But when Mississippi seceded and joined the Confederacy on January 9, 1861, the federal warship *Massachusetts* soon appeared on the horizon. Although fifty miles of coast were defended by only 1,000 Rebels with no earthworks or cannon, Ship Island Confederates nevertheless hung on through the summer, digging unexploded Union cannonballs out of the sand and firing them back at Union ships. But when Federal men-of-war arrived

Beauvoir, 2244 Beach Boulevard (1852). Planter James Brown built this raised cottage with square wooden columns with Doric capitals. It was bequeathed by Sarah Dorsey to Jefferson Davis in 1879, serving as the last home of the Confederate president. Now a National Historic Landmark, it was severely damaged by Katrina but is being repaired.

Magnolia Hotel, 119 Rue Magnolia (1847). Built as a luxurious getaway for the wealthy, the building houses the Mardi Gras Museum and is being repaired.

Biloxi Lighthouse, Highway 90 at Porter Avenue (1848). This is the only Southern structure ever to be draped and painted black to mourn the assassinations of Presidents Lincoln and Kennedy. It survived Katrina, as it has all other hurricanes, this time with only a slight lean caused by the storm's unprecedented surge.

Hermann House (Wood House), 580 East Beach Boulevard (1851). This home was built as a gift from French planter Peter DeBuys to his friend Adelaide Longer, wife of then-resident New Orleans cotton broker L. F. Hermann. The structure's raised basement, hip roof, five-bay gallery with fluted Ionic columns, and divided front stairs demonstrated the French influence. It was destroyed by Katrina.

in great force, the Confederates abandoned the island in the fall of 1862. By December's end, Biloxi, with its entire male population waging war in other theaters, had fallen into Union hands. The fort was damaged by Katrina, and its Ship Island lighthouse, a reconstruction of the antebellum original, was completely destroyed.

Biloxians passed the war free of many of the horrors endured elsewhere in the South. Battles were few, and those were usually minor naval encounters. Federal sailors engaged in no plunder of the town, and the people, even when lacking food and clothing, had general resort to experienced ship's-captains-turned-blockade-runners, who

Tullis-Toledano House (Woodlawn), 360 Beach Boulevard/ 947 East Beach Boulevard (1856). This home was built for New Orleans cotton broker Christoval S. Toledano and his wife, Matilde Clara Pradat, and acquired in 1939 as a summer home for New Orleans' Cotton Exchange president, Garner H. Tullis. It was destroyed by Katrina.

kept residents reasonably well provisioned. After Adm. David Farragut took New Orleans, Gen. Benjamin ("Spoons") Butler destroyed Fort Twiggs and built Fort Massachusetts, an impressive brick structure with vaulted ceilings, arched doorways, and inner courtyards. More than five thousand Confederate prisoners saw the insides of the fort's thick dungeon walls, including one housewife who was accused of inducing her children to spit on Yankee officers. One hundred and fifty-three Rebels died during their incarceration and were buried on the island. The fort was filled with mud by Katrina but is intact.

Prior to Katrina, Civil War-era Biloxi was recalled in Beauvoir and the Father Ryan House, which became the post-bellum residence of Fr. Abram Joseph Ryan, the "Poet Laureate of the Confederacy." Ryan wrote two poems, "Sea Rest" and "Sea Reverie," while overlooking the gulf from this house. He erected a cross in the heart of the front steps rising to his gallery, but after his death it was removed and a palm grew up through the steps, making the view of this stately structure even more "poetic." The Father Ryan House was completely destroyed by Katrina.

After escaping devastation during the war, Biloxi was ravaged by a yellow-fever epidemic in 1878, which claimed 45 lives out of a population of 2,000. Fire destroyed over twenty-five downtown buildings in 1889, and an 1893 hurricane wrecked 350 craft and took 2,000 lives along the Mississippi, Alabama, and Louisiana coasts.

Father Ryan House, 1196 Beach Boulevard (1841). This home was built by Natchez judge W. C. Wade. It served as the summer residence of New Orleans cotton factor John Watt and architect Thomas W. Carter and, later, as home of the Confederate chaplain, Fr. Abram Joseph Ryan.

On the positive side, ten miles of shell-paved roads were laid during this period, although the only beach road in Biloxi during this era was the one that a determined mayor built while objecting property owners were away in New Orleans. The resulting scandal was probably reported by the coast's newly founded and most significant newspaper, the *Biloxi Herald,* now known as the *Biloxi Sun Herald.*

However, the arrival of east-west railroad passenger service and the rise of the local seafood canning industry at Point Cadet in eastern Biloxi sparked an influx of tourism, which finally made a bustling city of the sleepy hamlet. Nowhere was this more evident than in the great hotels that sprang up at the turn of the twentieth century to accommodate summer visitors.

Like a scene from an old movie, the pirate-ship-shaped barge that was the Treasure Bay Casino sat stranded on the beach, pushed off her moorings by Katrina's storm surge.

These magnificent and bygone hotels included the White House (1894), formerly the Victorian residence of prominent jurist Walter White, and the $2 million Edgewater Gulf Hotel, designed by Chicago architect Benjamin Marsh in 1924 with a golf course and an artesian well that supplied 250,000 gallons of water to an Olympic-sized swimming pool. The Pine Hills Hotel was designed in 1926 by New Orleans architect Moise Goldstein, designer of Audubon Park, and the Buena Vista was erected in 1924 as a five-story, 200-room, stuccoed, Mission-style resort. The only remnant of that era is the Tivoli Hotel at 420 Beach Boulevard, built in 1927 by architect Carl E. Matthes, who had earlier designed the Buena Vista. This structure was severely damaged by Katrina and will likely not be restored.

Despite recurring hurricanes, the town grew rapidly after the turn of the twentieth century. The first Mardi Gras parades rolled in 1908 to the thrill of 8,000 residents, who also profited from the packing and shipping of 15 million cans of oysters per year. Seawall construction began in 1924, and the shell-covered beach road became paved Highway 90 the following year. When, in 1951, a 300-foot sloping beach was created and Highway 90 was four-laned, the Mississippi coast became home to the largest manmade stretch of white sand beach in the world.

The final push to modernity was, ironically, 1969's Hurricane Camille, which blew away the modest resort town with 200+-mile-per-hour winds, two twenty-five-foot-tall tidal surges, and over eighty deadly tornadoes. Thanks to the hardy spirit of its residents, Biloxi rose like a phoenix from the storm's rubble, replacing declining nineteenth-century Southern hotels with Las Vegas-style casinos such as the Beau Rivage, Hard Rock (replete with towering guitar-shaped sign), Treasure Bay (built in the shape of a gigantic pirate ship), and Biloxi Grand. By the year 2000, Biloxi had overcome 300 years of outrageous fortune to take her place among the top Deep South vacation destinations, while remaining at heart a hospitable, down-home place to live. Tragically, these structures were all severely damaged or destroyed by Katrina. Casino owners pledge to rebuild most of their damaged casinos.

Workers repair the exterior of the Biloxi Grand.

Beau Rivage Resort & Casino, 875 Beach Boulevard. This was one of Biloxi's eleven Las Vegas-style casinos. Large rooms with original artwork and marble-filled bathrooms, and a Riviera-inspired pool and an aquarium-surrounded restaurant, were highlights at Biloxi's finest resort casino. It was severely damaged by Katrina.

Architecture

Many of Biloxi's earliest-built homes evince French and Spanish influence in a distinctive coast vernacular style. The coast vernacular includes shotgun houses, straight or with lateral wings; the Creole cottage, with high, steeply pitched side gable or hip roofs, and a four-bay facade with two center doors (but rarely French doors) shaded by a roof overhang; and the Biloxi cottage, with a four-room plan and gable-on-hip or front gable roofs extending to cover a post-supported gallery and four-bay facade with two center doors.

The Scherer House is a Biloxi cottage, although it is a rare, brick, two-story version with even rarer stepped gables. Also known as the Spanish House, it is believed to have been built by a Spanish officer and was later owned by Charles Kaufman and Henry Fritz, two German cabinetmakers.

The Brunet-Fourchy House at 116 Rue Magnolia was originally built in 1835 in the four-room and two-chimney Creole cottage plan, but later acquired Greek Revival detailing, including a prominent iron railing. The Santini House at 964 Beach Boulevard was an early example of an American Cottage, with a center-hall plan and classically detailed entranceway with transom, sidelights, and flanking pilasters. It was destroyed by Katrina.

French Colonial-style houses included the Hermann House (Wood House) at 580 Beach Boulevard, with its divided staircase, and the Old Brick House, which graces Biloxi's back bay. This seven-bay structure was once owned by a man who directed the defense of Biloxi during the Civil War and who, briefly but single-handedly, held off would-be Yankee invaders with fake cannon. The former

Spanish House, 782 Water Street (circa 1840). This building has fifteen-inch-thick brick walls insulated with white sand. The stuccoed four-bay facade is made of oyster-shell plaster and features a two-story double gallery.

Old Brick House, 622 Bayview Avenue (1835). This building is more French or American than Spanish. Now a historic house museum, it was severely damaged by Katrina.

was destroyed by Katrina, while the latter suffered severe damage.

Greek Revival structures on Beach Boulevard included the wide-galleried Wade (Father Ryan) House, with its Ionic colonettes and French doors, and Beauvoir, of classical style mixed with substantial Georgian influence. Of these, only Beauvoir survived Katrina's 125-mph winds and twenty-five-plus-foot-tall storm surge at Biloxi.

Other architectural styles included the Colonial Revival, as in the Tullis-Toledano House, sporting fluted Roman Doric columns, a classical entranceway, and second-story accordion railing, destroyed by Katrina; the Robinson-Maloney House (1849) at 1042 Beach Boulevard, destroyed by Katrina; and the Redding House at 770 Jackson Street, which survives; the Neoclassical, including City Hall, which sustained minimal hurricane damage; and the Gothic Revival design of the Episcopal Church of the Redeemer (1873), destroyed by Camille in 1969 except for its tower, which was destroyed by Katrina and formerly faced the gulf.

Biloxi City Hall, 140 Lamuse Street (1920). The massive second-story portico is supported by Corinthian columns and features a denticulated cornice.

Culture

Biloxi remains a cornucopia of culture, offering theater, symphony, professional hockey, spectacular seafood, deep-sea fishing, competitive sailing, miles of white-sand beaches, championship golf courses, and gulf-view casinos. But as much as possible, the citizenry focus their activities around their historic structures, beginning with the Annual Gulf Coast Spring Pilgrimage, which presents tours of the region's surviving historic homes, churches, and gardens. The Father Ryan and Santini houses were bed and breakfast showcases before Katrina, while the Brunet-Fourchy House has been home to Biloxi's most renowned fine-dining establishment, Mary Mahoney's Old French House Restaurant. It reopened after Katrina despite serious damage. There, seafood lovers still dine in a courtyard surrounded by ancient, solid-brick walls or pause beneath the moss-drenched branches of the 500-year-old Patriarch Oak, damaged but still standing after Katrina.

Church of the Redeemer tower, Water Street and Beach Boulevard (1891). The tower was designed by Mississippi native and New Orleans architect Thomas Sully. Katrina brought great destruction here.

A sarcastic sign announcing the Spring Pilgrimage is tied to a tree outside a heavily damaged home along Highway 90.

Beauvoir, the last home of Confederate president Jefferson Davis, is scheduled to reopen in summer 2008, although Confederate Memorial Day beginning in April 2009 would be the best time to visit, when period speeches and music may be heard on the grounds. The Magnolia Hotel and the Old Brick House are now home to popular museums. These structures will also be repaired and restored.

Prior to Katrina, favorite neighborhood restaurants included Jazzeppi's Ristorante and Martini Bar just north of the lighthouse at 195 B, Porter Avenue, offering Italian food and drink in a romantic atmosphere, and the Ole Biloxi Schooner, downtown, where the po' boys rivaled those prepared in New Orleans. Both were destroyed by Katrina. Mary Mahoney's Old French House remains the top fine-dining locale, with divinely prepared lobster and flounder, while the Port House Restaurant in the Beau Rivage Casino will once again serve prime steaks with a breathtaking view of tropical fish and coral reefs in surrounding 10,000-gallon aquariums. McElroy's Harbour House Restaurant served gumbo, po' boys, and chilled oysters on the half-shell, but it was destroyed by Katrina.

Brunet-Fourchy House, 116 Rue Magnolia (1835). This may be Biloxi's oldest surviving structure. It is now Mary Mahoney's Old French House Restaurant and home to the 500-year-old Patriarch Oak. Both suffered severe damage from Katrina but survived.

Ole Biloxi Schooner, 159 Howard Avenue. Once famous for its po' boys, it was destroyed by Katrina.

Both Center Stage and the Biloxi Little Theater (founded 1946) offer live community theater, while the Saenger Theater at 170 Reynoir Street is home to the Gulf Coast Symphony. The Mississippi Sea Wolves play professional hockey at the Gulf Coast Coliseum, and the Ohr-O'Keefe Museum of Art at 136 G. E. Ohr Street displays the unique paper-thin pottery with brilliant glazes that was crafted by an even more unique native son, George E. Ohr, the "Mad Potter of Biloxi." All suffered damage from Katrina.

Barq's Root Beer, a coast original begun in 1898, is available anywhere soft drinks are sold in Biloxi. More adventurous souls may discover the famous Hurricane Hunter squadron at Keesler Air Force Base at 720 Chappie James Avenue. A heart-stopping film at the Maritime & Seafood Industry Museum at 115 First Street, which depicted Hurricane Camille's terrifying 1969 visit, was closed down by Katrina, which destroyed the museum. Dozens of fishing charters were available for deep-sea anglers before Katrina, many with interesting names such as *Happy Hooker, Reel Experience,* and simply, *Vamoose.* These or others like them will return to guide anglers to the gulf's great bounty.

Several longstanding traditions highlight Biloxi's cultural scene. Each year begins with the Dr. Martin Luther King Jr. Birthday Celebration and Battle of Bands parade from Howard Avenue to Lee Street, and Mardi Gras brings exciting Mardi Gras parades and balls from the Gulf Coast Carnival Association and the Krewe of Neptune. July brings an annual regatta courtesy of the Biloxi Yacht Club, and other locally held boat races run from April to September. On All Saints' Day, the descendants of original French settlers decorate the graves of their ancestors resting in the elaborate, above-ground vaults of the Old French Cemetery.

Christmas celebrations are popular in Biloxi, ranging from a celebration of past Christmases at the Annual Candlelight Christmas at Beauvoir (resuming in 2008), to the Annual Ethnic Christmas Trees of Tullis at the Tullis-Toledano House, where ten trees were annually decorated in the

A casino barge sits across Highway 90 atop what was the Holiday Inn near the Gulf Coast Coliseum. Katrina's storm surge pushed the floating casino several hundred yards from its moorings.

Biloxi's white-sand beaches have long been a favorite with both tourists and locals. They were severely damaged by Katrina, as was Highway 90, which runs along them. Both will come back, better than before.

Biloxi beach scene before Katrina.

traditional manner of the homelands of different peoples. The manor was destroyed by Katrina. The lighting of the city's beachfront Christmas tree and a parade of lighted boats cruising from the Broadwater Marina to Point Cadet have highlighted the annual Christmas On The Water Boat Parade, and surely will once again during future celebrations.

The Biloxi Shrimp Festival and Blessing of the Fleet has always been Biloxi's key festival, annually launching each shrimping season in May. The festival calls for a midnight mass at St. Michael's Catholic Church, a shrimp festival at Point Cadet, the crowning of the Shrimp King and Queen, and a trip to the Biloxi Small Craft Harbor at 679 Beach Boulevard, where a priest on a "blessing boat" sprinkles holy water on all passing commercial and pleasure boats. Undaunted by Katrina's unprecedented destruction, the people of Biloxi will continue to celebrate this festival so long as the industry itself survives.

Gulfport

Unlike Mississippi's other coastal towns, which were founded in the eighteenth and nineteenth centuries, Gulfport is a twentieth-century city and has put its own stamp on the area's history, architecture, and culture. With a soul more American than French, Gulfport was born of a union between the lumber industry and the railroad and has swiftly matured to become the coast's oceanic window on the world.

History

In the 1880s, Hattiesburg's founder, William H. Hardy, assumed control of the Gulf & Ship Island Railroad and selected present-day Gulfport as its southern terminus. But Hardy's dreams of a great lumber port on the Mississippi Sound were dashed by financial difficulties, and it fell to former Union captain J.T. Jones and his Bradford Construction Company to complete the railway to Jackson in 1900. Jones also widened the channel to the gulf, and when underwriters refused to insure ships entering the new port, he personally guaranteed the first ship's safety. With the *Trojan*'s successful docking, a great port city was born.

The port at Gulfport is Mississippi's window on the world. It suffered severe damage from Katrina but remains a viable port.

In 1906, 293 million feet of lumber, mostly yellow pine, were shipped from Gulfport, making it the largest lumber export city in America. The population grew to 5,000 practically overnight, and the town's first boom was launched.

Benton House, 14115 Rippy Road (1870). This home was built by Thomas and Melinda Benton, former slaves who helped found the Turkey Creek Community, which predated Gulfport. It is of the vernacular Gulf Coast Cottage style, with wood-frame construction resting on cinderblock piers.

W. J. Quarles Homeplace, 120 Railroad Street (1892). This house was built by Long Beach's truck-farming and education magnate and catalyst for the town's development. The vernacular style was altered by Hurricane Camille, which destroyed a lovely Eastlake-style porch.

African-Americans shared in Gulfport's prosperity, with a greater percentage owning their own homes than in any other Mississippi town.

Unfortunately, a 1906 tropical storm flattened a fourth of the standing timber in south Mississippi, so Gulfporters looked to truck farming and the tourist trade for their economic salvation. The elimination of yellow fever in 1905 opened the door to tourism, and the tranquil seas provided by barrier islands Cat and Ship offered fishermen abundant speckled trout, Spanish and king mackerel, redfish, flounder, red snapper, bonita, and tarpon from May to September.

Once again, the ever resourceful J. T. Jones seized the day, building one of the South's greatest early resorts, the Great Southern Hotel. This three-story vacation-mecca-on-the-water had its own power plant and artesian well, telephones and plumbing in every room, and a daily performing in-house orchestra.

In Long Beach, a few miles to the west, W. J. Quarles and Jim Thomas made their town one of the leading truck-farming centers in the United States, and the Radish Capital of the New South. A former teacher, Quarles also founded the Long Beach school system. His home is the town's oldest surviving structure, although it was damaged by Katrina.

However, one area on the western end of Long Beach failed to prosper. This was Pitcher's Point,

This gift shop on Highway 90 commemorated Camille and the many ships the storm deposited in downtown Gulfport. It was destroyed by Katrina.

Gulfport beach, Highway 90 at the Mississippi Sound, prior to Katrina.

named for the vicious leader of a band of pirates that preyed on Mississippi Sound shipping in the early 1800s. Before Pitcher was murdered by his own men for mistreating an Indian maiden, he placed a curse on them and their hideout. The curse apparently worked, as a home named Mount Vernon, a large hotel, and a Catholic school all built in the area either burned or were destroyed by hurricanes, until Camille completely leveled the Point in 1969.

Gulfport has been damaged by many storms, and as one Northern reporter noted, "Gulfport was churned into the sea" by a 1947 hurricane. But the town swiftly recovered in the 1950s, thanks to its large canning and shipping industries for salty oysters and little gray shrimp. Impressive beachside resorts, such as Mississippi City's Gulf View Hotel, treated tourists to easygoing Southern hospitality until two Las Vegas-style casinos, the Gulfport Grand and Copa Casino, helped establish the region, with its wave-swept islands and miles of white-sand beaches, as a key twenty-first century vacation destination. Although severely damaged by Katrina, Gulfport is rapidly moving toward recovery.

A trail of devastation and debris sat waiting for cleanup off Thirty-third Avenue in Gulfport after Katrina.

Architecture

Downtown Gulfport boasts several unusually interesting commercial structures, including the Gulfport Post Office on Thirteenth Street. One of Mississippi's finest examples of Second Renaissance Revival architecture, it was erected in 1910 as a two-story, hip-roofed, decorated-ashlar structure with seven window bays, three door bays, and a porch arcade of round arches carried on Doric columns. The eight-story Old Hancock Bank, built in 1928 at One Hancock Plaza, is of the Neoclassical style, while the two-story Old First National Bank Building at 1301 Twenty-sixth Avenue, severely damaged by Katrina, features a flat roof with parapet in the Beaux Arts style. The five-story Hewes Building at 2502 Fourteenth Street, built in 1905 in the Commercial Georgian Revival style, was listed on the National Register of Historic Places in 1982. These

Katrina flooding swamped this exit off I-10 in Gulfport.

structures suffered significant flooding during Katrina.

Gulfport-area residential architecture exhibits various twentieth-century styles. A rare exception was Grasslawn, built by Port Gibson surgeon and Louisiana planter Dr. Hiram Alexander Roberts. This Greek Revival, two-story structure was of pegged (not nailed) construction with hand-hewn, longleaf-pine timbers and cypress walls. Ten-foot-wide galleries on both floors were supported by ten two-story box columns with molded capitals and attenuated (thinner) bases. A large iron kettle on the front lawn was reputedly used to boil down gulf salt water during the Civil War.

The Dantzler House at 1238 East Beach Boulevard (Highway 90) was designed by Pass Christian architect Vinson Smith, Jr., for Bruno

Grasslawn, 720 East Beach Boulevard (1836). Gulfport's second built house, this was later owned by the city's first mayor, Finley Hewes, and was acquired in 1904 by John Kennedy Milner, who would one day own the Coca-Cola Bottling Company. Now owned by the city, it was destroyed by Katrina.

Dantzler-Fabacher House, 1238 East Beach Boulevard (1924). This home, erected by the son of a lumber baron, was subsequently owned by L. B. Fabacher, president and chairman of the board of New Orleans' Jax Brewery.

Griffin House, 426 Russell Avenue (1913). This home was built with wooden Ionic columns.

The Chimneys, 1640 East Beach Boulevard (1900). Built in monumental and classically adorned Colonial Revival style, this home was restored as a renowned fine-dining establishment before its destruction by Katrina.

Dantzler, son of Mississippi's largest lumber exporter, Lorenzo Dantzler. The clay-tile hip roof, overhanging eaves, and heavy brackets are indicative of the Mission style, of which this home is the coast's finest example. The house was severely damaged by Katrina.

Area Colonial Revival-style homes included the Chimneys in Gulfport, destroyed by Katrina, and the Griffin House in Long Beach, damaged by the storm. The former was built for T. G. B. Kellier with four, two-story Ionic columns supporting a central portico with decorative cornice, and a balustraded widow's walk on the peak of the hip roof. The front lawn was landscaped with rare fruit trees and lovely camellias before Katrina.

Long Beach's Griffin House was built by Methodist minister and pharmacist William T. Griffin as a "foursquare" house with Colonial Revival features. It was restored in the 1980s by Baptist-educated Church of Christ minister Terry Burgess.

Culture

Gulfporters still celebrate year round, beginning with their Krewe of Gemini Mardi Gras parades and the Shenanigan's St. Patrick's Day Parade. There's an Annual Deep Sea Fishing Rodeo on July 4th, which may move locations temporarily following Katrina, and fall brings Octoberfest, Mississippi's National Veterans Parade, and a Scottish Games and Celtic Festival. The Christmas Festival of Lights is Gulfport's concluding annual celebration.

Prior to Katrina, Gulfport boasted a wide variety of excellent restaurants. The Chimneys at 1640 East Beach served steaks and seafood among the Colonial Revival columns and camellia bushes, and at Vrazel's Fine Food Restaurant, the name said it all. The former was destroyed by Katrina, while the latter was severely damaged. The Blow Fly Inn, at 1201 Washington Avenue, was "where people swarmed for fine food" in a quaint building set on a cove overlooking pulchritudinous Bayou Bernard. Blow Fly Inn patrons enjoyed barbecued ribs, steak, and seafood on plates garnished with black plastic flies, while alligators observed quietly from a distance at dock's edge. Lil Ray's at 500 A Courthouse Road downtown served unbeatable po' boys, while the White Cap Restaurant at 1411 Twenty-eighth Avenue offered chilled oysters on

Great Southern National Golf Course offers beachfront vistas. This stately course was severely damaged by Katrina.

Vrazel's Fine Food Restaurant, 3606 West Beach Boulevard. Heather Radix helps clean up her father's restaurant. They planned to reopen.

The remnants of nice brick homes along Highway 90 in Long Beach lay broken and scattered after Katrina's storm surge.

the half-shell right over the water. In Long Beach, Chappy's Seafood Restaurant at 624 East Beach Boulevard offered coast vernacular "casual fine dining" a stone's throw from the beach. All were destroyed by Katrina.

Gulfport was heaven on earth for the young and young at heart before Katrina, offering a year-round Marine Life Oceanarium with trained sea lions and dolphin, and ferry excursions to Ship Island and Fort Mass-achusetts. Goofy golf, amusement rides, and water slides lined Highway 90, and the new Gulf Islands Water Park at 13100 Sixteenth Street offered eighteen acres of a nautical-themed water park with a Master Blaster water roller coaster. Sea-Doos, sailboats, and other nautical aids were rented along the beach, and charters for fishing and cruising were easy to find. Topping it off was the Lynn Meadows Discovery Center, one of the South's most outstanding children's museums. It remains to be seen which of these severely damaged or destroyed businesses will return after Katrina. Lynn Meadows Discovery Center is already under repair.

The Gulf Coast Coliseum at the Gulfport/Biloxi border will continue to offer professional ice hockey and concerts despite Katrina damage, while the Grand Casino and Copa Casino, which were washed from their moorings by the storm's surge, will likely rebuild. Sailing lessons will once again be offered at the town's Small Craft Harbor, and visitors to the University of Southern Mississippi's beachfront campus in Long Beach will once more pause beneath the Spanish moss-draped branches of Friendship Oak, the 50-foot-tall, 156-foot-limb-spread live oak that dates from 1487.

Marine Life Oceanarium before and after Katrina.

Lynn Meadows Discovery Center, 246 Dolan Avenue. This museum makes learning fun for children of all ages.

Friendship Oak, Highway 90, Long Beach.

Gulfport's Small Craft Harbor before Katrina.

Pass Christian

Represented on many ancient maps as "Passe aux Huîtres" (Oyster Pass), Pass Christian is named for an offshore channel that skirts one of the world's largest oyster reefs. Although some claim that the name "Christian" derives from a supposed explorer in Iberville's 1699 contingent named Christian L'Adnier, most historians believe the Pass was named for French exile Nicholas Christian Ladner, who arrived at Biloxi on the ship *La Marie* in 1719 and lived first in New Orleans and later on Cat Island. However, all agree that this charming coastal town is home to over a hundred ancient structures, including many lovely beach-view residences, that are listed on the National Register of Historic Places.

History

What is now Pass Christian (pronounced "chris-*chan*") was first home to generations of Native Americans who resided on the bay now called St. Louis, left several shell mounds in the region, and held councils near the towering Meeting Oak, which still stands east of the high school on West Second Street. The French came next, when in 1699 Iberville sent some of his party to locate a passage to Lake Pontchartrain. Royal cartographer Le Comte William Delisle explored the area and discovered Wolf River and Bayous Delisle and Acadian.

Madame Mezières received the first French land grant in 1717, and the Spanish granted land to the Asmand family in 1782. The Labat and Pellerin families soon followed, and in 1810, Gov. William C. C. Claiborne took possession of the region for the United States. The first public official appointed by the new regime was Philip Saucier, justice of the peace.

The first significant event in the region was the War of 1812. In 1814, 10,000 British soldiers arrived on the Mississippi Sound intending to reverse the American Revolution with a smashing victory at New Orleans. They captured Cat Island resident Juan de Cuevas and his wife, Maria, Christian Ladner's daughter, and offered Juan freedom, money, and future favors to tell them the best route to New Orleans. Cuevas

Ballymere, 551 East Scenic Drive (1839). The Creole cottage was remodeled in 1929 with the addition of a Colonial Revival inset gallery with chamfered posts sheltering a lengthy veranda.

refused and, after obtaining his release, sought out General Jackson and informed him of the English troops' movements. Edward Livingston, the lawyer who welcomed Jackson to New Orleans and helped him forge an alliance with his client, the pirate Jean Lafitte, later built a summer home on what is now Scenic Drive, the antebellum-home-laden road that parallels the beachfront Highway 90 for several miles.

Steamboat service arrived in the 1830s, as did one of the coast's greatest resorts, the Pass Christian Hotel. Ballymere, formerly the Pass's oldest surviving home, was erected in 1839 by Luciene LaBranche as a Creole cottage with exposed, beaded, hand hewn, cypress beams and beaded baseboards. It was destroyed by Katrina.

Creek Indians traveling west during their removal camped in the area for five months in 1837, and Mexican War hero and future president Zachary Taylor also visited the Pass in 1848. The South's first yacht club was formed at the Pass Christian Hotel in 1849, and many

Pass Christian Yacht Club. The organization was founded in 1849 as the South's second-oldest yacht club. The building was destroyed by Katrina.

of the town's lovely antebellum homes were constructed at this time. These included the opulent Blue Rose, the Greek Revival-style Harrison-Balter House (1849) at 849 East Scenic Drive, and the McCutcheon-Ewing House. All were damaged but not destroyed by Katrina.

However, in 1862, the 6,000 residents of this summer resort town suffered extreme deprivation during the Civil War. That year's Battle of Pass Christian saw the town shelled by Union gunboats until a housewife waved a white bedsheet from her upper-floor balcony and Lt. Col. Thomas Mellon's Third Mississippi Regiment ceded the town to 1,000 Connecticut infantrymen. This became locally known as the "Bedsheet Surrender." While Federal forces used the Saucier House as their headquarters during the 1862 occupation, starving locals boiled seawater for salt to trade for food from inland farmers. Yellow-fever epidemics further taxed the already struggling populace.

The war's end and yellow jack's demise precipitated the return of the tourist trade, the birth of the oyster-canning industry, and the 1883 erection of the coast's greatest resort, the $105,000, 250-room, three-story,

McCutcheon-Ewing House, 829 East Scenic Drive (1850). Built by Percival McCutcheon, this home was later owned by New Orleanian Isidore Newman II, president of the Maison Blanche department store chain, and Shreveport Times publisher John Ewing, who raised the Greek Revival structure to two stories in 1938. The brick steps with iron railings are pure coast vernacular.

Blue Rose, 120 West Scenic Drive (1848). This Greek Revival coast cottage features a steeply pitched, dormered roof and a now enclosed undercut gallery. Two lovely palms still grace the front lawn of the home, which was damaged by wind and storm surge from Katrina.

Saucier-Pratt House, 243 East Scenic Drive (1856). This home was built by Pierre Saucier, who lived on the upper floor with his family while the Greek Revival-style house was Union headquarters during the 1862 Federal occupation. It was destroyed by Katrina.

Queen Anne-style Mexican Gulf Hotel. The Inn by the Sea was a 1920-built beachfront hotel styled as a Mediterranean castle on seventy-five acres at Henderson Point. The Crescent Hotel at 126 West Scenic Drive, now a bed and breakfast inn, was the only surviving hotel from that era. It was severely damaged by Katrina.

Great homes usually accompany economic booms, and the magnificent Eastlake-style gingerbread home (1890) at 415 East Scenic Drive proves the axiom. Presidents Theodore Roosevelt and Woodrow Wilson were guests at the broad-galleried "Dixie White House" at 976 East Beach Boulevard (destroyed by Camille), and renowned newspaper writer Dorothea Dix built an elegant gingerbread cottage overlooking the gulf.

The twentieth century brought a decline in the region's seafood industry and tourism. In 1969, Hurricane Camille claimed sixty-five souls in the Pass and demolished the town. The Category Five storm leveled many venerable structures, including the Dixie White House,

Livingston summer home, Xavier Hall, Beaulieu, Ossian Hall, and the 1849-built Trinity Episcopal Church, where thirteen children, all of one family, tragically perished.

But the opening of Highway 90 and the creation of sand beaches in the 1950s brought a vigorous renewal of tourism. Pass Christian became a favored destination for sunbathers, yachtsmen, artists, and lovers of picturesque coast architecture and world-class seafood. Scenic Drive remains "one of America's most beautiful streets," and no one begrudges the Pass Christian Historical Society its claim that the Pass continues to earn its nineteenth-century nickname, "the Aristocrat of the South."

Katrina, with her 125-mph winds and thirty-plus-foot storm surge at Pass Christian, destroyed the downtown area just as had Camille thirty-six years earlier. Although many of the historic homes facing the beach were destroyed or severely damaged, and all were flooded, plans are already under way to rebuild the Pass in an architecturally sympathetic but considerably safer way than ever before.

After Katrina, a glass filled with muddy water still sat on a table outside what used to be a restaurant in Pass Christian.

Architecture

Early Pass Christian architecture included Greek Revival and Creole cottage structures altered to accommodate coast vernacular preferences. Greek Revival-style buildings included the McCutcheon-Ewing House at 829 East Scenic, with its elaborate Federalesque frontispieces and front steps with iron railings, and the Saucier-Pratt House at 243 East Scenic, with its inset gallery with four columns before six columns and a balustrade of cast-iron filigree. The latter was destroyed by Katrina and the former sustained flood damage.

Cottages included Ballymere at 551 East Scenic, built in 1839 as a two-room Creole cottage and given substantial Colonial Revival additions in 1929, but destroyed by Katrina, and the Blue Rose at 120 West Scenic, an 1848 coast vernacular cottage, which suffered severe damage from the hurricane. Other Greek Revival coast cottages included the three-bay Town Library at 221 East Scenic, built in 1853 as a residence and made a library in the 1890s, but destroyed by Katrina, and the Harrison-Balter House at 849 East Scenic, which is a vernacular Greek Revival raised cottage built in 1849 by Jilson Jarrison. This one-story, nine-bay, hip-roofed residence has an inset gallery with octagonal columns, iron balustrade, and marble front steps. Colonial Revival modifications such as double-leaf doors with beveled glass panels were added in 1905. The house was severely damaged by the 2005 storm.

The house at 706 West Beach (1985) was an example of a well-proportioned Acadian Revival residence, while the Stith-Morse House was vintage Colonial Revival before succumbing to Katrina. Built by the Stith family, and remodeled in 1950 by Stanford Morse, this home had a double-tiered inset gallery with Tuscan columns and turned balustrade, which are typical of the style.

Other prominent Colonial Revival structures included the Martin-McDiarmid House at 607 East Scenic, built in 1895 and remodeled in 1910 by master builder Frank Wittmann with a gallery and stylized Doric columns, and the Legier-Frye House, also erected by Wittmann with a hip-roofed

Stith-Morse House, 1024 West Beach Boulevard (1890). Built behind a grove of live oak, this home was once owned by Capt. Joseph T. Jones, the developer of Gulfport.

Legier-Frye House, 613 East Scenic Drive (1910). This home was built by the master builder of Colonial Revival houses, Frank Wittmann. The entrance porch and pilastered side solaria are each topped by roof gardens.

and lattice-enclosed, pergola-like entrance porch with roof gardens and a pergola porte-cochere. Both suffered extensive damage from Katrina.

Eclectic architectural styles also grace Pass Christian, and the best example may be The Castle, an aptly named Mission-style dwelling with a stepped parapet and offset circular tower. Two more examples are the Lake-Dennis Home, a monumental eclectic-style residence with a Spanish-tiled hip roof, bracketed overhanging eaves, and central bay defined by a flat-roofed, semicircular, Tuscan-columned portico, and the Perrier Home at 600 West Beach (1987), a Fred Wagner post-Camille eclectic design. Featuring five dormers and a lengthy inset gallery, front steps, and roof, it was erected on the site of what was once Louisiana governor John Parker's summer place. All of these homes were damaged by Katrina.

The Castle, 1012 West Scenic Drive (1922). This home was built by the owner, his daughter, and two helpers. It has received many additions and renovations since its construction. It was damaged by Katrina.

Culture

Pass visitors always loved to shop the downtown area, where art galleries and boutiques offered the creations of local artists and craftsmen. The Blue Skies Gallery (local art), Antiques and Interiors, and the Bazaar (the coast's largest indoor flea market) were favorites, as was the Hillyer House, which represented 175 creators of jewelry, pottery, and hand-blown glass. These shops were severely damaged or destroyed by Katrina, and it is unknown at this time whether they will return or be replaced by other businesses.

Before Katrina, The Harbour Oaks Inn (126 West Scenic) and Inn at the Pass (125 East Scenic) offered upscale bed and breakfast accommodations in historic houses, while eateries such as Annie's Restaurant (Bayview at Highway 90) and the Pirate's Cove (1321 East Beach) offered nightly chef's specials and New Orleans-style po' boys, respectively. Tigre's offered an impressive fine-dining experience, and the Chef's Market was a unique downtown food-sampling attraction presented every Friday from April to October. All of these

Hillyer House, 207 East Scenic Drive. Art galleries, flea markets, and boutiques abounded in the downtown area. This building was severely damaged by Katrina.

Pass Christian's once-thriving downtown business district was reduced to rubble by Katrina's storm surge.

structures were severely damaged or totally destroyed by Katrina.

The Pass Christian Historical Society's Annual Tour of Homes and the St. Paul's Carnival Association Mardi Gras Parade are spring highlights, as is the Annual Barbeque Under the Oaks, where diners enjoy barbecued ribs, Singing River bass, and whole roasted pig. Summer brings St. Paul's Catholic Church's Seafood Festival with crafts, games, and rides for the entire family, and a series of regattas sponsored by the venerable Pass Christian Yacht Club. And it's never too hot to try out The Oaks Golf Club, one of Mississippi's finest public courses. Fall yields Art in the Pass, showcasing regional creations, and the Annual Cruisin' the Coast Festival, with antique-car shows and beachside cruises. Christmas in the Pass features a Santa parade with marching bands and floats, strolling carolers, a lighted boat parade, and food sampling throughout the downtown area. While Katrina disrupted many of these festivals, all will return, as the people in the Pass are determined to rebuild their town and the good life they enjoyed prior to the storm's onslaught.

Pass Christian small craft harbor. It was severely damaged by Katrina.

Tigre's, 101 West Second. Located downtown, this restaurant offered Caribbean-style dining in the Pass. It was destroyed by Katrina.

Bay St. Louis

The great Choctaw chief Pushmata once wrote a poem about the bay he called Chicapoula, which went in part:"But if you ask me where the fairest and sweetest dream of bliss to woo; Ah, friend, in accents soft and tender, faint echo cries: a-chouc-pou-lou." He was referring to what in 1699 the French named the Bay of St. Louis.

The town on its western shores that borrowed its name is considered by many to be the garden spot of the gulf. A haven for vacationers and local artists alike, and the source of remarkable history and enticing lore, Bay St. Louis is a one-of-a-kind experience, even for the fabled Mississippi coast. Katrina's storm surge reached a record thirty-five feet

A large boat sat in what used to be a home off the back bay in Bay St. Louis, after Katrina.

at Bay St. Louis, demolishing much of the downtown area, crushing the beach boulevard in many places, and sweeping away many beachside historic structures. This did not stop folks from decorating surviving pine trees in their FEMA trailer parks with items recovered from the ruins of their homes and calling them "Katrina Christmas trees" in December of 2005. Nor did it prevent them from decorating the trailers with Mardi Gras wreaths or joyously participating in Waveland's annual Nereids Mardi Gras and St. Paddy's Day parades in early 2006. By springtime, area cars and trucks were sporting bumper stickers with the words, *Bay St. Louis—No Sniveling,* as residents gamely continued with their efforts to restore their beloved region to its former status as one of the most unique places on earth.

History

Toulme House, 218 North Beach Boulevard (circa 1856). This home stood where the French first placed settlers in the area a century and a half earlier. Frenchman John Toulme established the town's first mercantile store in 1812 and later served as mayor. The house was destroyed by Katrina; only its red-brick front steps remain.

Returning to Fort Maurepas from an exploratory trip up the Mississippi River, Iberville camped near the mouth of the Bay of St. Louis. The party "found a beautiful bay, which Bienville named Bay St. Louis, because it was on the day of St. Louis that we arrived there," André Pénicaut, their ship's carpenter and chronicler, wrote in his diary on March 30, 1699. "We hunted three days and killed fifty deer." They also hunted buffalo and were savagely attacked by mosquitoes, known to the Indians as "Marangouins." The next day, the French named a nearby barrier island Cat Island, for its omnipresent raccoons, which the Frenchmen mistook for felines.

Of the local Colapissa Indians, Penicaut noted that they tattooed their entire bodies; wore deerskins and antlers while hunting; worshiped idols in the shape of birds, dragons, snakes, and toads; buried their dead above ground; and dined on food cooked in bear fat. The French smoked the calumet with the natives and, with their help, placed in the area a contingent of a few families, a sergeant, and fifteen soldiers. This was the third settlement on the Gulf of Mexico after Pensacola and Ocean Springs.

Two members of Iberville's first expedition would produce many settlers in the region. They were cabin boy Jean Favre and Canadian woodsman Jean Baptiste Saucier, both of whom married "Cassette Girls" who arrived in the colony on the *Pelican* in 1704.

In 1721 the French gave a land grant of 17,000 acres to Madame Mezières, who established a colony on the bay. Former Parisian Jean Baptiste Necaise settled near the Wolf River and, like Saucier and Favre, would have many prominent coastal descendants. They would see the region fall into British hands in 1763, become annexed by the Spanish in 1780 (one year after Thomas Shields received a Spanish land grant west of the bay), exist for seventy-four days during 1810 as the Lone Star Republic of Florida, fly the U.S. flag on January 9, 1811, and wave the flag of the state of Mississippi in 1817.

By 1823, about 1,500 people inhabited the sandy flatlands near the Bay of St. Louis. They would meet a stiff challenge from the British on December 13, 1814, when one of the most important, albeit little known, battles in American history was waged in their region. The sleepy little village was attacked by British Admiral Cochrane and 10,000 combatants headed for New Orleans by way of the Mississippi Sound.

Several British barges armed with 1,000 men broke off from the armada and steered toward the bay on December 13. The small American schooner *Sea Horse* began loading stores of ammunition from the town's warehouse (located at present-day Ulman Avenue) to keep them out of enemy hands. As the British moved in at about 2:00 P.M., the townspeople of Shieldsboro (later renamed Bay St. Louis) prayed for the *Sea Horse*'s delivery.

According to legend, a visiting Natchez lady cried out, "Will no one fire a shot in defense of our country?" She then seized Mayor Toulme's cigar and set off one of the town's two cannon. An inspired *Sea Horse* crew turned to attack the British with a six-pounder cannon, and the British retreated to the cheers of the greatly relieved locals, who shouted to the *Sea Horse*'s crew, "Ask them to come back, Captain [William] Johnson. Say 'please.' We got lots of powder we ain't fired yet!" But when it became apparent that the *Sea Horse* could not escape, Johnson scuttled her to avoid her capture by the British.

The next morning, in the gulf due south of the town, seven American boats with 182 men, commanded by Lt. Thomas Ap Catesby Jones, engaged forty-five launches manned by 1,200 British marines with forty-three cannon under Captain Lockyer. The British suffered 300

Spanish Customs House, 707 Hancock (1787). This home was erected during Spanish rule. The town's oldest structure until 2005, it was built with four-bricks-deep, load-bearing walls and upper-floor galleries that originally spanned all four sides. It was destroyed by Katrina after surviving more than two hundred years of hurricanes and tropical storms.

casualties compared to the Americans' 60, but their overwhelming numbers ultimately prevailed. However, the Americans were the real winners, because the naval encounter delayed the enemy just long enough for Andrew Jackson and Jean Lafitte to ready their defenses to win the Battle of New Orleans a few weeks later.

Elmwood Manor, which stood at 900 North Beach Boulevard until it was destroyed by Katrina, was built in 1804-18 by Jesse Cowand, in the West Indies colonial style. He grew Sea Island Cotton on his plantation and served in the Battle of New Orleans with Capt. Thomas Beale's Company of Orleans Riflemen, on the extreme right of the American line near Lafitte and his buccaneers.

For decades after the War of 1812, pirates infested the Bay St. Louis area. The Pirate House in nearby Waveland, which was destroyed by Camille, was reputed to be the home base for Jean Lafitte during his final days. Pierre Remaux, the "King of Honey Island," operated along the Pearl River and pillaged ships in the gulf. What is now Buccaneer State Park in Waveland was once a secluded cove popular as a pirate hideout. The worst of the lot, the Copeland Gang, hid out in the Catahoula Swamp, plundering the locals for years until Copeland's 1857 capture and hanging.

The 1850s brought a short-lived prosperity to "the Bay," with Fr. Stanislaus Buteaux's founding of St. Stanislaus College as the oldest institution of learning on the coast. But the Civil War brought extreme deprivation to Bay St. Louis residents. A Federal blockade strangled the town, prompting a beloved local priest, Père le Duc, to regularly run the blockade in a schooner aptly named *Hard Times*. As Yankee raiders stole from the locals, the Monet family would hide their silverware and other valuables in a hollow oak near their home.

Bay St. Louis once again prospered in the 1870s by virtue of having the only shipping and railroad point south of Pearl River County, as well as many military roads cut through the area by Andrew Jackson sixty years earlier. It found further success as a fishing village with plentiful shrimp and oysters. Even so, its wild reputation continued, as prominent New Orleanians waged duels in the Bay well into the twentieth century.

The town of Waveland, adjoining Bay St. Louis to the west, was founded in 1888 and would eventually offer some of the coast's most inviting beaches. Kiln (pronounced "Kill"), a few miles north of Waveland, began to prosper after Samuel Favre, descendant of early settler Jean Favre and ancestor of Green Bay Packers quarterback Brett Favre, built an 1870s sawmill and general store in the area. Waveland's Gulfside United Methodist Assembly was established on the beach boulevard in 1924 to provide African-American families access to the gulf and beach during legally enforced segregation. The structure and

Monet-Breath House, 616 North Beach Boulevard (1818). This home was built by Judge P. C. Monet, who also served as mayor. This Queen Anne-style structure was the third oldest house in Bay St. Louis until 2005, when it was destroyed by Katrina.

pier were destroyed by Katrina, but the Gulfside Assembly area remains popular with groups supporting racial reconciliation.

The Bay St. Louis newspaper, the *Sea Coast Echo,* was founded in 1892. The Bay/Waveland Yacht Club was organized in 1898 and held its first annual regatta in August of that year. The club soon become the center of the region's social life and one of the nation's most competitive yacht clubs, being named as the National Yacht Club of the Year in 2004 by the U.S. Sailing Association.

In keeping with coast traditions, Bay St. Louis offered artesian wells and several large hotels, including the Crescent, Bay St. Louis, Clifton, Liberty, and Reed (now a nursing home), which drew wealthy New Orleanians vacationers to the Bay like bees to honey. In 1923, the town welcomed America's first step-type seawall, and when miles of

St. Stanislaus, 304 South Beach Boulevard. Founded as a college in 1854, it is now a Catholic high school for boys. It was damaged by Katrina.

South Beach Boulevard sat in ruins near St. Stanislaus after Katrina.

During the Civil War, the Monet family hid their silverware and other valuables in a hollow oak near their home, seen here after Katrina.

white-sand beaches were opened in 1950, the Bay began attracting both tourists and those who preferred laid-back coastal living. The arrival of NASA and the Stennis Space Center in 1963 ensured continued prosperity in the region, which even the devastation wrought by 1969's Hurricane Camille could not deter. Although those facilities were severely damaged by Katrina, they served as a haven for refugees and have been largely restored.

Camille's direct hit all but obliterated Bay St. Louis and Waveland, but small-town Southern hospitality continued to thrive in this area that is a mere forty minutes from New Orleans and thirty minutes from Biloxi. Katrina shattered downtown Bay St. Louis and wiped downtown Waveland from the map. A merger of the two towns is being considered, but regardless of the decision, the citizens of both towns will work together to rebuild their region.

A damaged vehicle atop the remains of a home in Waveland after Katrina.

Architecture

Before Katrina, more than 575 structures in Bay St. Louis were listed on the National Register of Historic Places or are located within designated historic districts. Two of those historic districts were almost entirely destroyed, while the others suffered substantial damage. The Beach Boulevard Historic District, which was hardest hit, offered Greek Revival, Queen Anne, Colonial Revival, Bungalow, and Mission-style homes with coast vernacular influence, and coast vernacular cottages with classical and Victorian influences.

Onward Oaks was a raised Creole cottage with a Greek Revival center hall, double pile plan (center hall/four rooms), and eclectic Victorian detailing typical of the Cottage Orné-type buildings erected on the coast following the Civil War. Recently restored by David and Marci Baria, it rested on brick piers and had undercut galleries spanning the front and rear elevations. Three dormers and the front gallery were reconstructed

A bowling ball was found nowhere near a bowling alley, in the middle of a sandy Main Street in Bay St. Louis after Katrina.

Onward Oaks, 972 South Beach Boulevard (1875). This cottage featured a steeply pitched, gable roof pierced by two brick chimneys and three gabled dormers with six-over-six double-hung sashes. The residence formerly served as Camp Onward, a New Orleans-based summer camp for children. It was destroyed by Katrina.

after Camille using historic photographs for accuracy. Katrina left only a concrete slab in its wake.

The Swoop Manor House was a good example of the Greek Revival cottage, while the Loeber House, built by the founder of New Orleans' Touro Infirmary, was a larger Greek Revival structure with Colonial Revival and Queen Anne additions. The Plauché-Gray House was an example of a Greek Revival House with vernacular idiom. Katrina's gigantic storm surge sucked all of these structures back out into the gulf when it receded.

The McDonald House is a good illustration of the local variation of the Queen Anne style. Built by local contractor Charles Sanger for William A. McDonald, this house has Queen Anne elements in its patterned shingles and bay windows but also offers coast vernacular features such as gables and delicate stick-work detailing. It suffered severe damage from Katrina.

The Haas House was an example of a massive Queen Anne residence. It rested upon stucco-covered brick piers and had a sloped gable roof and large triangular dormer with Palladian windows. Only steps and a concrete slab remain after Katrina's terrible onslaught.

The Otis/Green House was an eclectic structure originally built in New Orleans for the 1884 World Cotton Exposition in Audubon Park, loaded on a barge, and transplanted to the Bay. It had a jerkinhead roof, undercut gallery with Corinthian columns, and distinctive polygonal front elevation until Katrina completely destroyed the home.

Four examples of Beach Boulevard Historic District coast vernacular

Haas House, 712 South Beach Boulevard (1890). This debris is all that Katrina left of it.

Creole cottages are located in the 300 block of Main Street. These all have four-bay front porches and steeply pitched side-gable roofs supported by four wood posts with stickwork enrichment. Vernacular shotgun cottages with shingled gables are located on Ballentine Street, while shotguns with galleries are located on McDonald Lane. The shotgun house at 308 Main is a two-bay, galleried structure with a side porch and lateral wings. All of these properties suffered severe flood damage during Katrina.

Examples of the Colonial Revival style include Le Marin, on North Beach Boulevard, and the Carre House, several miles north of the Beach Boulevard Historic District. The Carre House was built by painter Paul Surcouf with a Palladian-motif window, shutters on the sides, slate roof shingles, and an undercut porch supported by rectangular wood columns with capitals. Le Marin was severely damaged by Katrina, while the Carre House suffered flooding damage.

Le Marin, named for the ship that brought the first French settlers to the region in 1699, was erected on land that was originally granted to Jean Baptiste Necaise. Its clapboard siding, gable roof, undercut gallery supported by wood posts, and central entrance with double-leaf doors are all elements of the coast vernacular interpretation of the Colonial Revival style.

Exceptionally attractive public structures include the county courthouse downtown and Our Lady of the Gulf Catholic Church. This church

Swoop Manor House, 414 South Beach Boulevard (1853). After Katrina, the red brick front steps are all that remain of this historic home.

Loeber House, 916 South Beach Boulevard (1850). This home was built in the Greek Revival style with Colonial Revival and Queen Anne influences, including side polygonal bay windows and a center shingled, pedimented, gabled dormer with turned balustrades and carved arch openings.

Plauché-Gray House (Marion Oaks), 806 South Beach Boulevard (1860). The vernacular style was demonstrated here in the gable roof, undercut gallery, wood posts with capitals, and center entrance with Greek Revival transom and sidelights. Dormers were added in 1940.

McDonald House, 502 North Beach Boulevard (1889).

was built to replace the original church founded in 1847 by Father Buteaux, who would establish St. Stanislaus College. Its stained-glass windows were made in Munich, Germany to depict events in the lives of Jesus, Joseph, and Mary, from the Annunciation to the Resurrection of Christ.

The Hancock County Courthousewas built by the firm of Keenan and Weis in the Neoclassical Revival style with a monumental portico and Ionic columns.

Otis/Green House, 418 South Beach Boulevard (1884).

This coast vernacular shotgun house (circa 1925, renovated 2004) was flooded by Katrina.

Carre House, 242 St. Charles (1895). The home was purchased in 1913 by Trudy Carre, who created the subdivision where it stands.

Le Marin, 406 North Beach Boulevard (1899). This home was built in the coast vernacular style, with a tin roof, gabled dormers, and seven-bay facade.

Hancock County Courthouse, 152 Main Street (1911). Damaged by Katrina, it is under repair.

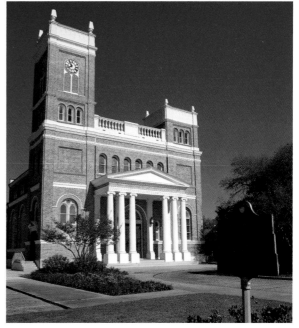

Our Lady of the Gulf Catholic Church, 228 South Beach Boulevard (1907). The structure was damaged by Katrina but remains largely intact.

Culture

The starting point for those interested in the Bay's history is the Hancock County Historical Society, located at 108 Cue Street in the Kate Lobrano House (1896), which was severely damaged by Katrina but repaired largely through the efforts of Society preservationist/historian Charles Gray. Those desirous of enjoying the good life in Old Town Bay St. Louis used to view the gulf and sample the seafood on the deck of The Dock of the Bay at 119 North Beach Boulevard, or walk across the street to enjoy the po' boys, steaks, and seafood at Trapani's Eatery, a family-run business since 1935. These properties were destroyed by Katrina, and only time will tell if they rise again.

Trapani's Eatery, 116 North Beach Blvd. This was home to the Bay's finest po' boys and other unexpected delights from the sea until 2005, when it was utterly destroyed by Katrina.

Before Katrina, the young and young at heart enjoyed choosing from a trio of interesting restaurants/pubs in the 100 block of South Beach Boulevard: the Fire Dog Saloon, Blue Parrot Restaurant, and The Good Life beachside bar. All were destroyed by Katrina. The Bay City Grill, at 136 Blaize Avenue, and Benigno's Grocery, 128 Blaize Avenue, just north of Old Town, survived Katrina and reopened within months after the storm. They offer some of the coast's best seafood.

In Waveland, Lil Ray's at 613 Highway 90, and J's Restaurant at 304-A Highway 90, offered that town's best po' boys until suffering severe damage from Katrina. Jack's Steakhouse, located in a humble shotgun house, served

Fire Dog Saloon, 105 South Beach Boulevard.

The Bay City Grill remains one of the Bay's most treasured eateries.

Jack's Steakhouse, 324 Coleman, was downtown Waveland's best steak and seafood restaurant.

fresh-from-the-gulf seafood such as Shrimp Bienville and Oysters Bordelaise and, not surprisingly, mouthwatering steaks, until it was swept away by Katrina.

Some of the coast's best shopping could be found in the Old Town Shopping District prior to Katrina. On the second Saturday of every month, shops remained open until eight o'clock, while live bands strolled the streets and mingled with shoppers seeking first-edition books, local objets d'art, and other regionally crafted gifts. Those tired of walking could rent a surrey on Main Street. Most buildings in Old Town were either destroyed, severely damaged, or flooded by Katrina. However, this did not long stop Bay residents from celebrating "Second Saturdays," albeit with tents and other temporary structures to house restaurants and sellers of books and objets d'art.

The Folk Art and Antique Museum, the former residence and studio of renowned local artist Alice Moseley, survived Katrina. During happier times, tourists flocked to see Moseley's video, *Hello, I malice Moseley*, and view her collection of colorful paintings with inspired names such as *Three Sheets in the Wind* and *Living High, Low and Middle on the Hog*. A reproduction of her work, *Pot of Gold*, by local high-school students, graced the wall of a shop at the corner of Main Street and Beach Boulevard until Katrina destroyed the wall.

A colorful art studio in a shotgun house, Main Street.

Pot of Gold.

Alice Moseley Home, 214 Bookter Street. This was home of the Bay's most famous folk artist.

Du Montluzin House, 208 North Beach Boulevard (1890). As the Bay Town Inn, it offered a view of the water a block from the Old Town art district until Katrina leveled it.

Prior to Katrina, accommodations could be had in or near Old Town in three excellent bed and breakfasts. These were the Heritage House Bed and Breakfast (1900) at 116 Ulman Avenue and the Palm House Bed & Breakfast (1893) at 217 Union Street, which survived Katrina with flood damage, and the Bay Town Inn, which was destroyed. The latter was erected as a home for Frenchman Ludovic du Montluzin, a teacher and onetime organizer of a Confederate company of French immigrants.

The St. Rose de Lima Catholic Church was built as an outgrowth of a school for African-American children begun in 1868. It is now home to the famous mural *Christus Sunsum,* on the rear and side walls of the sanctuary. The mural depicts an ancient live oak, draped in Spanish moss, with branches reaching out and encircling worshipers and a black Christ, who extends his arms heavenward. The altar was fashioned from driftwood trees washed ashore from the bay. Adjoining the church property is a lovely cemetery with above-ground vaults common to Mississippi's low-lying coastal region.

Sporting-inclined beachcombers could rent kayaks, sailboats, and bikes at Da Beach House at 604 Beach Boulevard after enjoying

Katrina's storm surge washed cars into the ditch along Highway 43 in Waveland.

St. Rose de Lima Catholic Church, 301 South Necaise Avenue (1926). It was flooded by Katrina but survived.

Chistus Sunsum mural, St. Rose de Lima Catholic Church (1927).

Favre monument in the cemetery beside St. Rose de Lima Catholic Church.

Casino Magic, 711 Casino Magic Drive, before and after Katrina.

Our Lady of the Gulf Crab Festival features amusement rides, some of the best seafood on the coast, and interesting twists on familiar games of chance, such as Crab Roulé in the Bay. The premises were severely damaged by Katrina, but the festival returned in July 2006.

Mural on downtown building depicting African-American contributions to the artistic community.

Hawaiian coffee in the café, or try their luck at Casino Magic, prior to Katrina. Da Beach House was demolished by the storm, and The Bridges, Mississippi's only Arnold Palmer signature course, located on site at Casino Magic, was severely damaged. Waveland's Buccaneer Bay Water Park at 1150 South Beach Boulevard offered waterslides and an outstanding wave pool for the truly young at heart. It remains to be seen which of these businesses will return after the hurricane.

Annual area festivals have included the Our Lady of the Gulf Crab Festival in July, where fair rides, art and crafts, and abundant seafood make everyone feel welcome, and the Diamondhead Arts and Craft Show in September, featuring one of the region's largest local crafts shows. The Bay St. Louis Little Theater provided fifty years of seasonal productions, including an annual spring dinner-theater production, a summertime children's theater program, and an annual Christmas production. As late as summer 2005, Waveland's Choctaw Four at Highway 90 and Highway 603 presented first-run movies and served hot buttered popcorn in a bag with ticket prices still reasonable at a mere two dollars.

While Bay St. Louis and Waveland, along with Pass Christian, bore the brunt of Katrina's wrath, the entire length of the coast endured high winds and a record storm surge that left the area in shambles. But neither Katrina nor any subsequent storm will dissuade coast residents from enjoying the good life they have built and rebuilt many times over the past three centuries. Their indomitable will is unbowed by this unprecedented natural disaster, and in the words of their state's greatest author, they will not only endure, they will prevail.